FRENCH CLASSICAL LITERATURE

FRENCH CLASSICAL LITERATURE

An Essay

BY

WILL G. MOORE

FELLOW AND TUTOR
ST. JOHN'S COLLEGE, OXFORD

OXFORD UNIVERSITY PRESS
1961

Oxford University Press, Amen House, London E.C.4

GLASGOW   NEW YORK   TORONTO   MELBOURNE   WELLINGTON
BOMBAY   CALCUTTA   MADRAS   KARACHI   KUALA LUMPUR
CAPE TOWN   IBADAN   NAIROBI   ACCRA

SET BY SANTYPE LTD, SALISBURY
AND PRINTED AND BOUND IN GREAT BRITAIN BY
W. & J. MACKAY & CO. LTD, CHATHAM, KENT

Foreword

THE following pages result from the give and take of college teaching and from the opportunity provided by the invitation to spend a year in the University of California at Berkeley. My first duty in making them public is therefore to acknowledge with gratitude the initiative of Professor R. N. Walpole, in extending to me such an invitation. To be transported from a university of seven thousand students into one of more than twenty thousand might have been a formidable experience. For me it was the discovery of a society determined to grapple with its vast problems, and of a body of teachers as learned as they were friendly.

Two of the debts which I incurred must find mention even in a brief foreword. The first is the kindness and care shown to my wife and myself by Ronald and Doris Walpole. Although carrying the administration of a large department Dr. Walpole found time not only to encourage the writing of these pages but to read the entire typescript. Where in particular I have avoided ignorance of the Middle Ages, I owe it to his wise counsel. Secondly I would acknowledge the courtesy and stimulus of the graduate seminar to whom these views were addressed. The members of 'French 218' have helped me more than any of them realised, and I hope that they may regard this little book as in some sense their own.   W.G.M.

CONTENTS

I

A CASE FOR REVISION

THE object of this essay is to hasten the end of a scandal. I mean the scandal of a literature officially praised and admired but in fact pre-judged and neglected. Is it not scandalous that in schools and universities, in lectures and textbooks, in examination papers and study programmes, French Classical literature should be proclaimed as the finest product of a nation's culture, and that by all too many who read them the actual works should be thought artificial, affected, unexciting and old-fashioned? Boileau once said that the effect of great literature was not persuasion, but conviction and surprise. We have forgotten that he thought so, and have unjustly labelled him a pedant. Nor have we applied his criteria to the literature of his age and country. French critics themselves have not encouraged us to look for these qualities; they have spoken of order, rule, and perfection, and have suggested that we may admire but should not enquire.

We who are teachers carry the main responsibility for this state of affairs. It is we who have written the histories of literature, the editions with their introductions that contain much biography and hardly any aesthetics. It is we who have directed researchers to explore the 'influence' of any and every writer on others but have kept them off the main problems of the seventeenth century. It is we who have thought to explain so startling a social and literary phenomenon as modern classical drama by talking of rules and conventions and unities. The student who asks what these features have to do with the originality inseparable from any work of art has been too often sent away empty. To judge by what textbooks say of the principle of imitation of the ancients one can only conclude that seventeenth-century writers must have been very unoriginal. 'Classical' indeed for my generation at the university meant unexciting, formal and frigid.

It is a curious fact that the notion of perfection ascribed to classical literature discouraged research, and without research any critic could use what superlatives he liked. The whole field still suffers from this lack of critical attention and control: a masterpiece of comedy can be called a satire, simply because the domains of comedy and satire have not been patiently worked out and established. Basic research has still to be done on the assumptions, methods, mental outlook, of the chief artists of the period. This is not the case in any other period, I think, of any modern literature. When he confronts a poem by Lorca or Mallarmé or Goethe or Hopkins, the student is expected to know that that poem attempts to solve a particular problem, achieves a unique creation, which is the proper object of study and enquiry. This is not often suggested, and hardly ever worked out, for the poems of La Fontaine, the Maximes of La Rochefoucauld, or the tragedies of Racine. So the neophyte may be excused for thinking that there is no depth or personality in classical literature: it was a matter of imitation and keeping to the rules. Yet it was Molière who said that it was more important that literature should be enjoyed than that it should be correct.

M. Daniel Mornet spoke for many of us when he said that, as taught to him, 'l'histoire de la littérature française de l'époque classique était d'une harmonieuse simplicité. Contre des écrivains sans goût et sans bon sens s'étaient dressés d'abord Malherbe, puis Boileau et ses amis . . . deux blocs opposés l'un à l'autre . . . les études, très rapides et très superficielles, laissaient dans l'ombre toutes sortes de problèmes essentiels.' Mornet's book was written precisely to show that this simplicity is an illusion, that converging studies have now allowed us to see the background of classical literature as complex and contradictory. He, and M. Adam after him, have put the rich literary production of the time in some sort of scientific perspective.[1] We no longer need to think of the plays of Corneille as a school of heroism, and of moral instruction in fine attitudes, but as a form of entertainment, which had to satisfy the demands of actors and audiences. This left little room for the poet to air his particular doctrines, even assuming that in the manner of a modern he might wish to do so. When M. Lanson suggests to me that Corneille shared the views of his Polyeucte, I must see if that is his opinion, or a fact established by evidence.

On Boileau, when recent enquiries into particular aspects are pieced together, the old picture is seen to be quite impossible (and by the 'old' picture one means what is found in the books and still taught in the schools). The work of M. Charles Boudhors, of M. Adam, and now of Mr. Brody, makes it impossible to go on thinking of a school of poets working out Boileau's view of literature,

[1] D. Mornet, *Histoire de la littérature française classique,* 1947. A. Adam, *Histoire de la littérature française au 17e siècle,* 1949.

and impossible also to think of Boileau as a man who said in the *Art Poétique* his whole view of poetry.

Yet recent research has achieved something: it has shown that much the greater part of the literary production of the age was not classical, was the reverse indeed of classical. Much more popular at first than the works we know as classical were sentimental plays, artificial poems, immense epics and fantastic novels. They are legitimate products of the time as Racinian tragedy is, and more representative: 'The classical age is thoroughly classical only to those who refuse to consider more than a portion of the facts,' wrote Lancaster. Does this leave much content in Faguet's statement: 'C'est l'esprit du 17e siècle que nous appelons proprement l'esprit classique fran-çais.'?[2]

If the picture is new, do we not need a new word for it? Some scholars indeed suggest that we can do without the term 'classical', a heritage from an uncritical epoch. They would describe Racine's plays more properly as 'baroque' or 'the theatre of reason'. Unless we were prejudiced, they say, we should find in them a sense of unrest, of question-ing, rather than a sense of repose and of calm. The question is certainly open, and the following pages can offer no hard-and-fast solution. I have no assurance that what I see in classical literature entitles me to be dogmatic on its intention or its essential features. I want only to advance the debate by bringing into consideration what scholars have discovered, which is (I believe) of sufficient novelty and interest to renew subjects that in textbooks and teaching have become threadbare and unprofitable. To use the word 'classical' does not mean that one is in the

[2] H. C. Lancaster, *A history of French dramatic literature in the 17th century*, 1936. E. Faguet, *Drame ancien, drame moderne*, p. 35.

least precluded from discerning baroque elements. Perhaps the end of this essay, rather than its beginning, is the place to look for any attempt to infuse a new content into an old word. For the moment, it seems preferable to use the word classical in its traditional sense, as referring to that outburst of creative writing that occurred, largely in Paris, in the sixth and seventh decades of the seventeenth century. In bulk it was a tiny portion of what was then written and read, just as it was addressed to an extremely small part of the population. Yet it possessed an appeal to the discerning that ensured its constant republication, in contrast to ephemeral works which contemporaries liked as much or more, but which are now forgotten.

Its emergence in that milieu and at that point of time is difficult to explain. It would seem to owe something to the evolution of French society, something also to new forces at work on French intelligence, in particular the work of Montaigne, and to the new science. Several of its features are found in works of undoubted quality produced in the preceding decades, so much so that scholars have invented the term 'pre-classical' to describe the work of such men as Balzac, Chapelain, Voiture, and Rotrou. Lanson, who not only wrote the first modern history of the movement in his 'classic' manual of 1894, but who all in all is perhaps the ablest mind that has given itself to the methodical study of literature, saw affinities between the mind of Descartes and those of the chief classical artists among his contemporaries. Others, with less justification, have tried to explain the respect for order in classical literature by the growing stability of the French monarchy; they see Richelieu as an architect of classicism, no less than of absolutism. Such parallels are apt not only to mislead but to stray beyond the evidence. All that historians of literature can do is, in the words of a contemporary scholar who has done more than most to reveal what was happening in this most complicated period, 'expliquer la genèse et l'évolution de ces styles en les replaçant dans un large contexte historique'.[3]

The broad historical context is an essential point, since it is admitted that literature owes its development in great part to the historical situation in which it is born. But the situation of French classicism has been seen much too narrowly. The growing sense of order and unity seen in the development of the French monarchy is not perhaps the main feature at all. This order was an answer to disorder. The French classical writers all lived through the Fronde, which used to be thought a comic war, a ladies' war, but of which French historians now speak as a series of tragic years, as momentous and as confused as those of our own Civil War. They speak of French society as threatened by individualism and anarchy: 'une société qui tend à se diviser en sous-classes . . . voilà le spectacle que donne la France en 1661, spectacle de division totale qui résulte du jeu des privilèges, de la faveur et surtout de l'argent. Il n'y a pas un lieu d'ensemble'. If this is the picture we should be seeing, then the Roi Soleil appears in a very different light from the pleasure-loving megalo-maniac castigated by Lavisse. Perhaps, as the latest history of the period suggests, the forces unleashed by the Renaissance were so various and conflicting that on all sides arose attempts at stabilization, at holding things together, in the state, in the church, in society, in thought and in the arts. This is in fact the plan suggested by Roland Mousnier in his treatment of the sixteenth and

[3] V. L. Tapié, *Baroque et classicisme*.

seventeenth centuries in the *Histoire Générale des Civilisations:* a crisis in economics, politics, and morals, countered by a multiple effort of resistance: 'la lutte contre la crise'. In this general wave of stabilising forces, classicism appears as one among many others, such as Jansenism and absolutism. But the historians also remind us that these abstractions are the names we give to tendencies that we fitfully discern; they do not describe the way things happen. We should not for instance imagine Louis XIV and his advisers pursuing a well-thought out policy of centralization: there was rather constant wavering and uncertainty of the way forward, or even of the way out of a pressing situation: 'deux politiques contraires . . . elles ne cesseront de se combattre'.[4]

Literature is usually written by people sensitive to the world of thought round about them, and if we are to see the literature of this period in its right and broad context, as Tapié suggests we should, then we must look at the context of ideas no less than of politics. Why, for instance, have we never asked ourselves how far French classical literature is what it is because it was produced in the midst of a scientific revolution, within a society where the discoveries were as startling and the discussions as animated as in our own; where to the intelligent, the traditional picture of the universe was seen to be more and more untrustworthy and new thought seen to be more and more inevitable? The whole moment, the ferment of interest in upper middle class French and Dutch and English society, has been described by Butterfield and Dingle, but such books as theirs are not thought necessary

[4] P. Sagnac, *La Formation de la société française moderne,* 1945, p. 49. R. Mousnier, *Le 16e et le 17e siècles.* (Histoire générale des civilisations, 4) 1954.

for the study of French literature.[5] The reason for this
vacuum is not far to seek; we find it in the accepted notion
of classicism. Since French classicism was understood to
be the result of calm reflection on truths unaffected by
time or place, then there was no need to think that
French writers of the mid-century were conscious of the
world of ideas in which they moved. One has only to
look at the facts to see that this is an impossible assumption. Pascal was a leader of the scientific movement. La
Fontaine even brings his interest in science into the
Fables. Passages of Molière are almost inexplicable if we
think their author had no interest in contemporary ideas.
It is grotesque for us to imagine the keenest minds of the
day having, and showing, no interest in the intellectual
debates going on around them.

What is the outstanding feature of life in the seventeenth
century, as we can see it from contemporary memoirs,
pictures, letters, and documents? Not order or rule or
reason, not pageantry or splendour, but vigour and even
violence, restless activity. Aldous Huxley has caught it in
his account of Père Joseph; it was in his master Richelieu
no less. The life of a churchman like Bossuet, far from
being one of stately dignity as suggested by his prose, is
one long series of discussions, disappointments, negoti-
ations, in the desperate and apparently tireless attempt to
impose Christian standards and orthodoxy upon an age
determined to be rebellious. The life of Fénelon was no
more peaceful. Nor that of Saint-Cyran, or Vincent de
Paul. Pascal died at thirty-nine (a victim of disease and
still more perhaps of the ignorance of his doctors) after a
life of immense and controversial activity. Molière died

---

[5] H. Butterfield, *The Origins of Modern Science*, 1949. H. Dingle, *The
Scientific Adventure*, 1952.

exhausted at fifty-one, not from composing 'great' works, but from an almost daily struggle to keep a theatrical company in existence. Racine lived his first forty years, during which almost all his poetry was written, in a fever of conflicting energies. The social pleasures of even such people as La Rochefoucauld and Madame de Sévigné must have formed a very small part of an existence that we now know included constant lawsuits, money difficulties and journeys that would daunt most modern travellers. These are not exceptional cases. Travellers to France were impressed by activity everywhere, building, trading, travelling, new towns, new industries, even in the religious houses a mass of business and affairs that took up time and personnel. If such was the mark of ordinary existence, what must the daily life of the energetic have been, of a Louvois, 'lui qui était', said Mme de Sévigné, 'le centre de tant de choses', of an Arnauld or a Bayle. To read Taine we might think that the lazy existence of a courtier was typical, and no doubt life was boring for the privileged, at times: one remembers the marquis in Molière who spent his day spitting in a pool to watch the ripples. To the writer and the public who laughed at this *bon mot* the point probably was that their day could not be less like that.

So it is a fiction to imagine that the calmness and repose which we may see in classical art corresponds to the conditions in which it was written. It was not the classical writers but the Romantics who wrote from an ivory tower, or might be accused of doing so. The calm of classical literature, in so far as it exists (and I think it does, though we have seen it because we looked for it) is an achievement, a reply to violence, and to chaos. (Is not any work of art a reply, a reaction to a situation?) It is something very different from what students have been told, for example in these lines:

Rien d'inquiet ou de tourmenté; aucun trouble, aucun malaise. Tous les écrivains sont contents de leur époque . . . les auteurs classiques considèrent le monde comme un ensemble de rapports déterminés . . . dont la complexité n'a rien qui les trouble.[6]

Such statements are an indication of how far tradition may impose upon good judgment. None of them would occur, I suggest, to an unbiassed and critical reader of the writers they purport to describe. They occur only because the official explanation insisted on in French education is that *Romantic* means warm, personal, real, in distinction, contrast, conflict against *Classical*, which means cold, general, artificial. It is time, high time, that the whole argument were abandoned, or stated in terms that correspond in some degree to the facts. I think that a Marxist scholar, for all his bias, has come much nearer to these facts than the oft-reprinted manual of M. Pellissier:

Les apologistes du classicisme n'ont vu qu'ordre, clarté, perfection, là où il n'y eut en fait que malaise, paradoxe, confusion, crise larvée . . . où par conséquent la perfection de la forme fut, par rapport au contenu, confus et fuyant, à la fois une conquête durement gagnée et en échappatoire.[7]

I hope that the design of this essay on French classicism is now becoming clear. I have no startling new interpretation to offer. For myself I am content to go on thinking of the leading French writers of this period as 'classical'. I do not wish to substitute another category, and then make the authors conform to it. Rather the contrary.

[6] G. Pellissier, *Le Mouvement littéraire au 19e siècle*, 1895, p. 3.
[7] H. Lefebvre, *Pascal*, 1949, p. 92.

Without preconceptions, but taking the contemporary evidence fully into account, I want to ask what this 'classical' literature is really like, what in the light of recent research it looks like. I shall try to describe what these authors seem to be attempting. My excuse for doing this, and no more, is that in teaching on these lines I have found that well-known works, when restored to what seems to have been their original context, are freed from accretions of interpretation: they are liberated as works of art. The element of surprise and shock and risk, which belongs to every successful work of art, is restored to them. We have tended to force into an academically constructed mould, so to speak, works which indeed share a common spirit, but which are less uniform, less impersonal, less universal perhaps than we have accustomed ourselves to say and to think.

The remedy for this state of things is, as I see it, to submit these works to fresh scrutiny, to use the material that has been discovered: manuscripts, variants, contemporary discussion, in order to get as near as we may to the original intention of the writers, interpreting their work within the 'wide historical context' which Tapié enjoins upon us, and remembering that this context is one of ideas and habits of thought, no less than of social forms and class outlook. This means that we keep in mind that such a controversial work as *Tartuffe* was written in an age when the attitude of scepticism was new and attractive, strong perhaps in the very circle in which Molière moved, but an age also in which the power of the church and the authority of religion were much stronger than they are to-day. This is therefore a case where we may easily attribute to a writer of comedy views which it would have been folly for anyone in 1664 to express.

The new path is not easy to tread and one may stray off it at any point. The real danger of the student of literature is, I am persuaded, anachronism. He tends always to interpret the event in the light of later developments. Here we touch a vital difference between the creative writer and the historian. The writer may claim to 'imitate' nature or the ancients, but as R. C. Knight has pointed out, he does so in a work of art only at the cost of 'anachronismes constants et flagrants'. For 'l'anachronisme est la condition même de tout art vivant'.[8] Many scholars forget this: they treat Racine's plays about Greek myths as if they were Greek plays, which they are not. Recent research suggests that probably Racine did not even imitate the Greek playwrights, in the first instance. But the anachronism necessary to the artist is fatal to the historian: Racine might write a seventeenth-century play about Iphigenia, but we must not read his play as having the same assumptions and outlook as shall we say a play by Goethe or by Anouilh. An American scholar has put the point neatly: 'it is the humble use of scholarship to ensure, as far as its knowledge extends, that when we read the poetry of three centuries ago, we attain the poet's meaning.'[9]

Two points may complete this introductory discussion. First, writers never consciously set out to write the literature that makes them famous. I do not think that any French classical writer made it his conscious aim and intention to write 'classical literature'. We should not need to make this obvious point were it not that the books about these things suggest almost the reverse. Yet as far

[8] R. C. Knight, *Racine et la Grèce*, n.d., p. 404.
[9] J. Pommier, *Aspects de Racine*, 1954, p. 184. Austin Warren, *Crashaw*, preface.

as we can see Racine wrote *Phèdre* for the same reason as Molière wrote *Le Bourgeois Gentilhomme* and La Roche-foucauld his *Maximes*, that is: in order to treat a certain 'matter' in a way that would please their more critical contemporaries in the theatre or in the salon. Racine indeed said in his preface that he had striven to achieve a work that was 'raisonnable', which we may translate, I think, as something like: satisfying, convincing, not obviously far from the truth. Molière, as M. Bray shows him at work, year by year, almost month by month, as actor manager, must have had a quite materialistic bread-winning purpose in writing each play, under conditions of hurry and strain and pressure. That does not mean that the resulting work of art contains no classical features, for in all these cases it plainly does.

This brings us back to the first point made in the introduction, the narrow compass of what was known and considered literature. Most French classical literature escapes what theorists call literature. It contains, as we shall see, little lyric or epic poetry. Its greatest works are innovations, extensions of the boundaries of what was then called literary. The *maxime*, the letter, the sermon, the portrait, these did not really belong to literature until the French classical writers had produced their work. Racine's tragedy and Molière's comedy are both quite original new departures from traditional types; in effect they are new genres.

We need not regret these things: they take nothing from our enjoyment, they rather enrich it. The finest products of literature, as of education, are its by-products. The greatest works are never written as great works but to satisfy a particular object: was not Leonardo da Vinci commissioned to cover a stretch of wall in the refectory of Santa Maria delle Grazie? It is incidentally that great works slowly emerge from the mass of contemporary production. There must have been many French men who thought with Bayle in 1677 that '*l'Hippolite* de M. Racine et celui de M. Pradon sont deux tragédies fort achevées'.

II

THE PURSUIT OF POETRY

THE seventeenth century would have seen no sense in this heading. They knew what they meant by poetry; it was abundantly cultivated all round them, and there was no need to seek it out or pursue it. For them all literature was poetry. The distinguishing literary medium was verse. The various kinds of literature were the forms of verse. To be a poet was to write in verse and poets were the only true men of letters. Such a writer as Montaigne, for all his wit, did not write literature in the sense that most people understood it: 'L'art littéraire, au 17e siècle, c'est la poésie.' One might perhaps say that prose was considered by theorists to be an exercise, poetry an art.

The literary handbook of the Renaissance was Aristotle's *Poetics*. Its modern, chiefly Italian, interpreters, argued endlessly about the kinds of literature therein treated; very little was said about the possibility of literature developing new kinds. We do well to remind ourselves that much of the literature on which the fame of the *grand siècle* rests is new literature in this sense, and much of it in prose: the epigram, the letter, the sermon, the

portrait, the new comedy, and the new novel. All these
ways of writing were either re-invented or given totally
new scope by the French classical writers; none of them
were discussed by Aristotle. It is strange that we think of
their works written according to rule, since there were no
rules for anything but poetry:

> La doctrine classique ne s'occupe que de la poésie, c'est-à-
> dire des genres qui chez les anciens étaient écrits en vers:
> épopée, tragédie, comédie, genres mixtes, poésie lyrique,
> bucolique et satirique, voilà son objet; joignons-y le roman
> pour ceux qui l'apparentent à l'épopée. Par doctrine classique
> nous entendons la poétique.[1]

It is one of the strange reversals of literature that so
productive an age, that practised poetry so much and
thought of it so highly, should be famous for almost
everything except its poetry, and that French classical
poetry should be to-day thought of as second-rate and
almost insignificant. We can see some poetry, but in the
greater prose writers. When La Fontaine and Racine
are referred to as great poets, we assume that what is
meant is the skill of the one as a fabulist and of the other
as a dramatist. Yet Molière in his day was called a poet.
Let us look into this matter. Why is it that our pursuit of
classical poetry takes us into drama, and into prose?

There is a serious misunderstanding here, which is only
partly explained by the fact that our conceptions of
poetry have changed since 1600: between us and the
French classical writers stands Romanticism, often spoken
of as a liberating movement, but which seems in this
respect to have narrowed conceptions of poetry to that
kind which was personal, emotional, non-intellectual,

[1] R. Bray, *La Formation de la doctrine classique en France*, 1927, p. ii.

imaginative. It was against this narrow view of poetry as the expression of emotion that Mr. Eliot and the modern classical critics made their case. Many people, because they find no lyrical poetry in French classical literature, do not trouble to look for any other kind of poetry.

Yet poetry was cultivated in France at that time, more energetically than any other form of writing. There is overwhelming evidence of the popularity of poetry throughout the seventeenth century. A great deal was published, and even more lies in the larger manuscript collections, copied by patient amateurs who thought it too good to destroy. M. Lachèvre spent a lifetime collecting and indexing the French anthologies of the period. Of one of the more popular of these he says: 'Les poésies réunies par les soins de Charles de Sercy ont fait les délices de ses contemporains.' The *Recueil* in question appeared first in 1653 as *Poésies choisies de Messieurs Corneille, Bensserade* (plus fourteen more names) *et plusieurs autres*. A Second Part appeared in the same year, a Third in 1656, a Fourth in 1658 and a Fifth in 1660, each one of over 400 pages and each several times reprinted. In this mass of verse is there no poetry? It is poetry of a kind, in the Renaissance or Petrarcan tradition, elegant and pleasing in form, monotonous in content, using *ad nauseam* an artificial stock of expressions that certainly once gave pleasure. It is the poetry of wit, of escape, or of fancy. Escape from a world in many ways harsh and crude and ugly and all too realistic (a world described by Aldous Huxley more vividly than by most historians), must have been something sweet, a pleasant pastime. Such poetry did not need, and was not intended, to convey emotion; it played with concepts, broidered conceits and tirelessly varied the jargon of rhetorical love. The fetters of attachment, a glance or even a lock of hair, these subjects delighted seventeenth-century poets no less than those of the previous century. Here is one example out of hundreds:

> Ne dis plus, cher Tirsis, que mon bonheur extrème
> Te va faire envieux de ma condition;
> Si tu savais aimer de la façon que j'aime,
> Tu connaîtrais quel mal cause ma passion.
>
> Je dirais toutefois devant Caliste même
> Que son beau sein n'est pas mon inclination,
> Ce n'est point pour son teint que l'on voit le mien blème
> Et je n'ay pour ses yeux qu'un peu d'émotion.
>
> Sa bouche dans mon cœur n'a point porté de flamme,
> Ses mains n'ont point donné de liens à mon âme,
> Cependant je languis et je sens mille feux,
>
> Et celui que Tirsis croit plus heureux qu'un Ange
> Destiné pour périr d'une façon étrange
> Comme un autre Absalon est pris par les cheveux.

This is not real literature, it is Renaissance small coin, imitation of imitation, written no doubt with no great design, just for the pleasure of making or reading verse, and in pursuit no doubt of real poetry.[2]

For the finer spirits were in no doubt that true poetry is more than this. Chapelain's letters for instance show us a man who thought highly of Malherbe, and of the discipline of exact writing that he had imposed, but who was not afraid to say that he thought him ignorant of real poetry: 'Je vous dis qu'il ignorait la poésie . . . c'était

---

[2] To see how far this triviality is from true poetry we have no need to come forward in time and quote the Romantics. French poets on the eve of the seventeenth century were writing verse of which their successors seemed to know little but which modern scholars have compared to Donne. e.g. Sponde: Tout s'enfle contre moy, tout m'assaut, tout me tente, Et le Monde, et la Chair, et L'Ange revolté. . . .

un borgne dans un royaume d'aveugles.' Rapin, in a treatise published in the same year as Boileau's *Art Poétique*, speaks of the majesty, dignity, and mystery of real poetry. This sort of thing La Bruyère found in the new tragedy, that gripped the heart and hardly allowed the spectator to breathe. Racine speaks of the true pleasure of tragedy as a kind of dignified and triumphant melancholy, a poetic emotion in fact. Boileau himself, whose versified rules of verse delighted salons in 1670 and when published became the chief European handbook of poetry was under no illusions that poetic heights were beyond him, the critic 'plus enclin à blamer que savant à bien faire'. His work on Longinus had taught him that poetry may have the sort of effect that we today associate with lyric poetry: 'il enlève, ravit, transporte'.

As a satiric poet Boileau wrote some of the most realistic verse of the day, yet he would have agreed with the writer of the sonnet just quoted that there must be a sharp division between the actual and the imagined. As the language of daily life is natural so the language of poetry must be artistic, that is, full of *art* or *techné*, unnatural. The natural in art was a difficult concept to entertain, because along with the natural came idiosyncrasy, excess, burlesque, bombast, the turgid, and the incomprehensible. Boileau's war against all these things is evident in the *Art Poétique* and it is no less clear that his audience approved his view. Nature, as Longinus again had taught him, could be a foundation of art but never a method.

It would be interesting to study the limits of the natural in French classical art. Both painters and poets admitted nature as part of their picture. But even in comedy, where nature could be most freely expressed, Molière was concerned to impose order on his material. In the Fable,

La Fontaine was no less concerned to enforce the *moralité* which he called 'the soul of the story'. In *Psyché* he explains why in describing some things verse and not prose must be used:

Au lieu de passer par les airs et de se servir de son char et de ses pigeons elle entra dans une conque de nacre attelée de deux dauphins. La cour de Neptune l'accompagna. Ceci est proprement matière de poésie: il ne siérait point à la prose de décrire une cavalcade de dieux marins; d'ailleurs je ne pense pas qu'on pût exprimer avec le langage ordinaire ce que la déesse parut alors.

> C'est pourquoi nous dirons en langage rimé
> Que l'empire flottant en demeura charmé . . .

In the *Fables* he discovered more subtle ways of fitting prose and poetry: he uses exact and prosaic notations of behaviour and observation and escapes into poetry at will.

The eighteenth century was to show to what aridity this concept of art might lead. But we should not think that Renaissance poets practised it out of petulance or pique. It was perhaps the only way open to them whereby a poetic world might be preserved at all. They could not foresee that other influences would combine to dry up the springs of personal expression. This is not the place even to sketch what happened. Was it because of dislike of individualism that rule and regularity were adopted as essential to the discipline of art? Or the other way round? Great intellectual activity seemed to put a premium on clarity and wit, even in poetry. The Cartesian spirit indeed has been blamed for the eclipse of poetry, and the claim is worth hearing when expressed by a student of Wordsworth:

Cartesian thought enforced the growing disposition to accept the scientific world-picture as the only 'true' one. The criterion of truth which it set up, according to which the only real properties of objects were the mathematical properties, implied a depreciation of all kinds of knowing other than that of the 'philosophes'. And as both religion and poetry (whatever may be our conception of them) spring from quite other modes of knowing, the Cartesian spirit, in so far as it prevailed, was really hostile to them both. Descartes himself is perhaps only the most conspicuous representative of a way of thought which was irresistibly gaining ground as the century proceeded, and we must not therefore ascribe to him all the consequences of that thought. But the fact remains that by the beginning of the 18th century religion has sunk to deism, while poetry had been reduced to catering for 'delight', to providing embellishments which might be agreable to the fancy, but which were recognised by the judgment as having no relation to reality. . . . The Cartesian spirit made for the sharper separation of the spheres of prose and poetry.

According to M. Adam, the influence of Gassendi and the fashionable scientific academies of the forties and fifties in Paris was even more powerful in quenching poetic enthusiasm. 'On ne fait pas des lyriques avec des pyrrhoniens. Des hommes comme Chapelain et Costar peuvent bien affirmer la primauté du langage poétique sur le discours. En fait, tout le poids du mouvement intellectuel tend à étouffer l'élan poétique.'[3]

Nor was it only the philosophically minded who stood in the way of poetry. Many serious people seem to have thought it, as they did the theatre, a waste of time, or worse. We know how Port Royal angered Racine by suggesting that a writer of plays was an 'empoisonneur

[3] B. Willey, *The Seventeenth Century Background*, 1934, p. 87. A. Adam. l.c., 299.

public'; a contemporary manuscript reference suggests they were equally hard on the 'pastime' of poetry: 'MM. Arnauld et Nicolle n'approuvent pas qu'on s'occupe tant à faire des vers: sunt verba et voces. Il est impossible de raisonner en vers. On y est trop contraint, cela gêne trop.' This alliance against poetry of puritanism and pedantry is significant, I think, of the age. Sainte-Beuve's ironical picture of M. de Saci would have surely included this gem, had the critic known of its existence: 'Les poètes sont les apôtres et les maîtres de l'amour propre. La poésie est l'art de mentir. Ce ne sont que des mots. Il y a peu de chose à apprendre dans les vers.'

There was then dislike of poetry among many cultured people, as well as several strong forces that tend to make the production of light verse easy and the pursuit of true poetry difficult in the later seventeenth century: the tendency towards order, the resistance to individualism, the new science and the new philosophy. I think we must add one more not often mentioned but explained by no less an authority than M. Mornet, with great clarity, in his history of French Clarity. This was the tradition of Rhetoric in French education. He suggests that it is impossible to overestimate the influence over three centuries of writing of the way in which, at school, boys were taught to comment and compose, to develop 'lieux communs' (not in the modern sense of banalities but the application of the right arguments and expressions in description of any scene of history or mythology. The first composition that Diderot remembered being set in school was to imagine a speech by the serpent that would persuade Eve to eat the apple). This inculcated, according to M. Mornet, a sense of the fitting, the generally applicable, the orderly division of points in a speech which are to be found on a high level, but still rhetorically, in French tragedy and poetry.

La poésie a été d'un seul coup condamnée à n'être qu'un fantôme de poésie. Les scrupules de style ont achevé ce qu'avaient commencé ceux du choix et de l'ordonnance des idées.[4]

When due weight has been given to all these factors, we may well feel that we have accounted for the absence of great poetry in the literature of French classicism. This is a widely prevalent view and one object of this chapter is to challenge it as being both erroneous and confused. We may not find the sort of poetry that Romanticism or our Anglo-Saxon tradition has accustomed us to look for, but that is a very different thing. We like the natural and the personal in poetry, and these qualities we can find in some degree in the French classical writers. But suppose they wrote poetry containing quite different qualities, suppose that these artists had found a way of poetic expression that was intellectual rather than emotional, ornate rather than unadorned, human rather than individual, then would it not be stupid for us to say: all that is not real poetry? Would we not really be saying: that is not in my tradition of poetry? This is in fact very much what has happened. It is illustrated by a volume called *The Claims of French Poetry* by John Bailey, now chiefly known because of the devastating reply that it evoked from Lytton Strachey in *Books and Characters*.

In matters of poetic taste there is no authoritative answer and no final court of appeal. Seventeenth-century people, or the French now as then, may find poetic what

[4] D. Mornet, *Histoire de la clarté française*, 1929, p. 239.

to others seems the opposite. But this means that students of literature should tread carefully. It should give us pause, for instance, that intelligent Frenchmen find great poetry in their classical movement, and that for them Racine and La Fontaine are not exceptions to the spirit of their age. Have we noticed such a passage as the following?

S'il y a quelque chose en notre poésie qui, pour l'ampleur du sujet, pour l'ondoiement des contours et de la flamme, pour les *mâles appas*, réponde aux belles pages de Bossuet, il ne faut le chercher que dans Molière. Que ne s'est-il rencontré un génie de même race pour remplir et peupler d'égale sorte l'autre sphère, celle du pathétique et de l'idéal, la grande poésie française était créée.[5]

Let us then start to look at French classical poetry afresh. We may well begin with Boileau, a satirist, since the natural and the concrete found refuge in satire.

Looking at the first drafts of his early satires (recently made available with Prof. Adam's valuable commentary) we see at once that we have to do with a man pursuing poetry with energy. There is more pamphleteering than poetry, especially at first when Boileau is more or less a hack writer for a certain coterie, but there is no doubt about the vigour. As M. Adam has said: 'Les idées de Despréaux sont celles mêmes du cercle auquel il appartient. Il n'est personnel que par la vigueur et l'intransigeance du ton, la fermeté de l'expression. Ses haines les plus sincères sont empruntées.'[6] The idea is in Juvenal but the expression is enjoyable, and the picture vivid, of this poet (probably Tristan l'Hermite) who was sick of his ill luck in Paris:

[5] Sainte-Beuve, *Port Royal*, Pleiade ed. p. 280.
[6] A. Adam, *Les Premières Satires de Boileau*, 1941, p. 136.

Las de perdre en rimant sa peine et son bien,
D'emprunter en tout lieu et de ne gagner rien,
Sans habits, sans argent, ne sachant plus que faire . . .

so leaves the city in disgust, the city of swindlers is not for him:

Je ne sais point en lâche essuyer les outrages
D'un faquin orgueilleux qui vous tient à ses gages,
De mes sonnets flatteurs lasser tout l'univers,
Et vendre au plus offrant mon encens et mes vers:
Pour un si bas emploi ma muse est trop altière.
Je suis rustique et fier, et j'ai l'âme grossière;
Je ne puis rien nommer si ce n'est par son nom,
J'appelle un chat un chat et Rolet un fripon.

This is good verse. Is it not poetry, of a kind? M. Lanson suggests that Boileau has the gift of being picturesque and entirely unsentimental:

Il n'y a dans sa poésie ni sentiment ni passion, ni roman, ni drame, ni comédie. Cela est purement pittoresque; ce n'est que la réalité fortement, fidèlement, sérieusement rendue. Il y a vraiment dans Boileau un Hollandais . . . l'expression est si propre, si serrée, si objective, qu'aussitôt on a le tableau devant les yeux.[7]

Yet Boileau seems to have been less fond of the concrete object than of the pungent phrase. He is a master of formulae that sum up an attitude. Some of his lines are as resonant and as attractive as the Maximes of his great contemporary, no wonder they are so quotable, and so often quoted:

Qui ne sait se borner ne sut jamais écrire . . .
Ce que l'on conçoit bien s'énonce clairement . . .
Un sot trouve toujours un plus sot qui l'admire . . .

[7] G. Lanson, *Boileau*, 1892, p. 62.

Boileau delighted in being personal and knew that his strength lay in denunciation:

> Je ne puis pour louer rencontrer une rime . . .
> Mais quand il faut railler, j'ai là ce que je souhaite,
> Alors, certes, alors je me connais poète . . .

Apart from satire it is his criticism that made his reputation, with its curious ups and downs. Recent research has shown how little well-thought-out doctrine there is in the *Art Poétique*, but it was not for nothing that it was a salon success. The vigour and point of the writing is remarkable. His views are those of his intelligent contemporaries, but his expression is individual and poetic, witness his defence of the grand style in the epic:

> Que Neptune en courroux s'élevant sur la mer,
> D'un mot calme le flots, mette la paix dans l'air,
> Délivre les vaisseaux, des syrtes les arrache;
> C'est là ce qui surprend, frappe, saisit, attache.
> Sans tous ces ornements le vers tombe en langueur,
> La poésie est morte ou rampe sans vigueur.

The view of Boileau and his work that is gradually emerging from recent research makes the old anthologies of his work quite out of date. His great services to poetry are in fact quite other than what used to be called his merits. He was not really, it now appears, a 'législateur du Parnasse' at all but (as Dryden testified) a vigorous and yet perceptive poet and critic. He did not hold the pedantic view long ascribed to him that good sense and reason make a poet, but he spent much time translating a famous treatise of Longinus that asserted the opposite. It was this translation that started all the 18th-century discussions on the Sublime, which were a factor in the

formation of Romanticism. Not only so but Boileau's
last poetic effort seems to have started a new and critical
form of light verse. La Harpe once said that 'lorsqu'on a
prétendu que Boileau n'avait ni fécondité ni feu ni verve
on avait oublié *Le Lutrin*.' It is a pity that space allows
no quotation from this excellent work, but any who will
may test Boileau's powers, for example in the battle of the
books described in the Fifth Canto, which probably
inspired Swift.

'The last refuge of the concrete,' says a recent scholar of
French poetry in this age, 'was in the Baroque universe of
the Libertin poets, but La Fontaine's poetry was to show
that there were, for the classicist poet, still possibilities.'[8]
Over a wider poetic field than Boileau, for satire is only a
minor ingredient in his work, and with finer imaginative
insight, La Fontaine succeeded in writing poetry that kept
a place for the concrete and the everyday, while never
being trivial. It is indeed one of the marvels of French
literature that in an age of rule and convention, when
expression of opinion was frowned upon in the work of
art, there should be a great poet who out of the material
of everyday life could so constantly create poetry which
his contemporaries enjoyed. Legends have grown about
both the man and his work; the one was thought a
wastrel and a philanderer, and the other a haphazard and
spontaneous product of luck or insouciance. Both views
are unsupported by the facts. The poet, as his correspondence is there to prove, was certainly unpractical but
neither lazy nor happy-go-lucky in matters of poetry. He
not only read very widely, both ancient and moderns,
but spent much time on the pursuit of poetic perfection,

[8] Odette de Mourgues, *Metaphysical, Baroque and Précieux Poetry* 1953,
p. 246.

as much on a short as on a long poem. His cultivation of the naive and the unsophisticated is a device of artistic communication, and not at all the expansive and thoughtless unburdening which we have too easily assumed. The apparently careless reflection is preceded by planned workmanship and long meditation. As Rousseau said, though for a different reason, this is not for children. The chief French poet of our own time tells us why:

Prenons garde que la nonchalance ici est savante, la mollesse étudiée; la facilité, le comble de l'art. Quant à la naiveté, elle est nécessairement hors de cause: l'art et la pureté si soutenus excluent à mon regard toute paresse et toute bonhomie.

Again the task of expounding the ways of genius is too delicate to be methodically attempted here. As far as one can put it succinctly, La Fontaine's poetic technique seems to have been to meditate on suggestive texts and attitudes, the former usually from an author he knew very well, followed by close work on both poetic setting and a restricted and delimited poetic subject. It is not irrelevant, I think, to note that his subjects are largely situated in one of two realms. They belong either to mythology or to the animal kingdom. This gave him the immense technical advantage of being able to describe either without being entirely ordinary and trivial; neither domain came into the purview so to speak of daily living. He was thus free to introduce into his poetry echoes of the everyday because his subject was always something other than the limited and concrete life of the real world, in a larger and vaguer setting. Thus in *Adonis*, which we might consider as the first masterpiece of classical French poetry, he has a theme which any reader will regard as out of this present world. To develop it as if it really happened is therefore something of a poetic paradox. Moreover he is free to broider on Ovid and Marini in such a way as to convey in graceful numbers what he seems to admit is an improbable idyll but which seems in his hands to have singular power of suggestion. We notice not so much the person, or the Act described, as the gesture, the mood, the sound and the flow of the language. What seems to be a haphazard list leaves the impression of a quintessence:

> Jours devenus moments, moments filés de soie,
> Agréables soupirs, pleurs enfants de la joie,
> Vœux, serments et regards, transports, ravissements,
> Mélange dont se fait le bonheur des amants . . . .

A wistful comment is to be savoured without precise enquiry as to the circumstances:

> O vous, tristes plaisirs où leur âme se noie,
> Vains et derniers efforts d'une imparfaite joie,
> Moments pour qui le sort rend leurs vœux superflus,
> Délicieux moments, vous ne reviendrez plus.

As Valéry again says: 'Il ne faut pas s'émerveiller de la grande simplicité de ces héros, les principaux personnages d'un poème ce sont toujours la douceur et la vigueur des vers.'[9]

This simplicity as a means of conveying moods and reflections can make a new book out of the *Fables* for any who have read them only as material to be recited, or as stories with a tiresome moral attached. The very choice of a mean subject (for animals in that age had no dignity or importance compared to man) allows almost complete freedom of treatment: the lines may be short or long, *enjambé* or self-contained, the remarks loosely or closely

---

[9] *Variété*, II. 78.

attached to the subject, provided the whole be sensed as a unified reflection, as something *fondu*, to use Proust's word. I used to think that the charm of La Fontaine lay in the personal asides and confessions ('the lyrical bits', as an undergraduate once called them) in *Les Deux Pigeons* for example, or in lines such as these:

> Si j'osais ajouter au mot de l'interprète,
> J'inspirerais ici l'amour de la retraite:
> Elle offre à ses amants des biens sans embarras,
> Biens purs, présents du ciel, qui naissent sous les pas.
> Solitude, où je trouve une douceur secrète,
> Lieux que j'aimai toujours, ne pourrai-je jamais,
> Loin du monde et du bruit, goûter l'ombre et le frais?

I still think that the occurrence of such passages is one of the delights of reading French poetry, but I was surely wrong to pick on these and the like as *the* poetic or the most poetic parts of the work. The poetry, I believe, is in the larger context, in the roving inspiration. If we take cases that seem to give us glimpses of how the poet went to work, it turns out to be not with the aim of self-expression in the sense of the above passage, or in any Romantic sense, but rather with the aim of absorption to the point of expressing to the full the poetic suggestion inherent in the chosen subject. To take one such simple case: we know by his own revelation that he wrote I.16 after I.15, and he also tells us why he wrote *La Mort et le Malheureux*: 'Je composais celle-ci pour une raison qui me contraignait de rendre la chose ainsi générale.' So the *general* aspect of the little poem was intentional. All is, in fact, if we look at it, generalized. The subject is a man without a name, 'le malheureux'. In unadorned terms he calls for death to remove him from his cruel lot, which is not further specified. His request is answered, death comes, knocks, enters, appears to him, and he recoils in horror at 'the object' that actual death presents. As any man would, he asks for more time:

> N'approche pas, ô Mort. O Mort, retire-toi.

This is all, but for a tailpiece in praise of Mecenas who said he would submit to any mutilation if he might still live. This reflection is found in two of the poet's favourite books, Seneca's letters to Lucilius and the last essay of Montaigne's Second Book. It seems likely that both were used in the long meditation which the reflection would need in order to be worked up in this metallic and impressive form.

In the 1659 edition of the *Essais*, the Latin of Seneca is not only quoted but translated in the margin, ending with the words . . . 'pourvu que je vive', and the point of the passage is enforced by the cases of Tamburlaine and Antisthenes. One would hesitate to imagine La Fontaine writing without both Seneca and Montaigne in mind: it is the sort of poem that *might* be the result of appreciation of Montaigne's essay. What seems at first sight to be a versified *lieu commun* is more likely to have been a carefully meditated 'moment' which seemed to the poet sufficiently 'general' to become matter of art.

Do we not observe a similar process in the creation of *Le Lion devenu vieux* (III.14)? The trivial subject, available to the poet in both an ancient and a modern collection of fables, required (one would think) lively detail in the narration. The poet's concern has been, apparently, to remove much of the detail. Words in his source that he did not use are: jouet, vil, affaibli, abandonné, gisant, dernier souffle, boutoir, pointe, perça, broya, front, ruade. He has kept some general, suggestive or euphonious terms: antique, souffrir, atteintes. The blows are related repetitively and flatly (coup), not distinguished as in the source. Suggestive words are added: terreur des forêts, prouesse (for prestige), in one case as a paradox: devenus forts par sa faiblesse. The tone is altered by an affective plural: aucunes plaintes, and by giving to the ass (an object of derision) alliterative protection.

Quand voyant l'*Ane* même *à* son *Antre Accourir* . . .

The resulting vignette is memorable, elegant, suggestive, bodiless; it conveys, not an incident, not what once happened, so much as an attitude, in this case of animals but interesting in itself, a sort of picture of dying greatness. So Jean Schlumberger gave to his study of the last years of Retz this title: *Le Lion devenu vieux*.

There seem to be no rules for this poetry. Elegant sounds and expressions abound, the sense of surprise is constant and itself a recovery of fresh and spontaneous enjoyment that is absent from most poetry of the time. The apparent irrelevances of La Fontaine have never been studied; they are material for the diagnosis of poetry rather than of psychology. A recent enquiry into *La Fantaisie de Victor Hugo* might suggest a companion volume from which we should learn some poetic secrets: the poetry seems to depend on the reverie, the constant escape from daily contingency, a temperament that is inconstant, *volage*, in things of mind and spirit, yet at the same time remorseless in its concentration on the presentation of an impression. With such subjects the trivial and the monotonous seem to be unavoidable, yet are always avoided. The moral, which in most cases would stifle the poetry, seems to be the gate to the general, poetic suggestion which delocalizes, extends, universalizes the incident. No other poet so constantly and so informally associates the local and the ordinary with the fleeting, the vague, the incorporeal, and the intellectual. The political allusions are almost worth a study on their own. They are 'passionately expressed', says one editor. Surely not, nor coherently as material for action, but on occasion, suggesting a connection which only a man of culture and humanity would make. They were apparently part of the reverie to which the 'subject' of the poem gave rise. That 'subject' is no longer interesting, only its product, its quintessence.

Such a poem as *Un Animal dans la Lune* (VII.18) seems to have no single thread. It consists of forty lines of reflection on the reliability of sense impressions, then a dozen lines which relate an amusing case of this from the Royal Society of London, finally eighteen lines of reflection on the happy state of the English people, free to pursue the arts of peace, and an appeal to the English King to negotiate peace for France. So the 'fable' proper occupies one fifth of the matter. In itself it is most enjoyable: the comic aspect of the learned men puzzled by a monster far away that turns out to be a mouse in the machine, *lune* getting mixed up with *lunette*, this is the delightful heart of the poem, but not the whole poem. Yet one feels the poem is not a letter that may stop when it will: it has a unity. Is the unity in this fleeting linking of two different reflections to a case, suggesting both insight and humour, on a scientific subject, how in science we may get things right or get things wrong, or have no leisure to indulge in such cultural activities at all? As one tries to explain, one is in danger of writing a prosy moral that hides the poetry.

Perhaps a last example from the last book of *Fables* may suggest a continuance of the same manner of writing. *Le milan, le roi et le chasseur* (XII.12) is dedicated to the Prince de Conti on his approaching marriage. It opens with thirty-five lines of praise for his qualities that are not shared by all the great. Then the story of a hawk presented to a king, which settles on the monarch's nose and could not be dislodged, but the royal patience stood the test. Then thirteen lines of reflection that the Indians would take such a bird for a transmigrated ancient soul. Then, 'another way' of telling this kind of tale. In this case the bird clawed the hunter's own face, and everyone laughed. Even a Pope might have laughed; laughter is gods' delight,

> Que le peuple immortel se montrât sage ou non
> J'ai changé mon sujet avec juste raison . . .

for perhaps a hunter's stupidity is more worth rebuking than a king's patience is worth praising. Again the charm seems to lie in the easy leap from point to point, as if irony could span any details of human action, or of animal action that is so reminiscent of human attitudes.

La Fontaine is probably the only classical French poet still read with pleasure, and as these notes on his work have shown he is not an easy or straightforward poet to understand. In a way he is useful to study alongside his less gifted contemporary Boileau, since both suggest how arduous in such an age and society the pursuit of poetry had become. Together they give us the only durable poetry of a most gifted group of writers, the only poetry, that is, that stands in its own right. For we must not forget that much of the poetry that could not find fit expression in lyrics found its rhetorical but magnificent expression in drama. It is therefore partly covered in another chapter, but something should be said of it here, to complete the outline of classical poetry and to raise at least the difficult question of how far the French classical dramatists succeeded in going beyond rhetoric to poetry. It is a question that possibly nobody but a Frenchman could answer. Voltaire certainly felt the greater plays of Corneille to be poetry: he was not just using that word to mean versified drama. I think we can still understand this feeling though we may not share it.

Yet to find out precisely where the poetry lies in the complex rhetoric of French classical drama is a task as yet unattempted and towards which these pages can make only the most tentative and individual contribution.[1] Research has shown that seventeenth-century playwrights were not concerned to write their feelings or opinions, but to write a play that had sufficient dramatic material to fill five Acts and to please an audience. In writing out their play they could allow themselves rhetorical passages, indeed they were encouraged to do so by the actors themselves, who liked bombast. Let us not forget in this connection that none of the speeches in French classical drama were recited as we like to hear dramatic sentiments recited. When Molière attempted this he ran up against the impossible. Speeches were declaimed in a sing-song manner; we might almost say they were intoned, and this no doubt had its influence on those who had to write the speeches.

At what point does rhetoric allow poetry? Not necessarily, as in Hugo's plays for instance, where it becomes emotional or personal. Here again we may be

[1] In grateful acknowledgement of the trail blazed by E. Vinaver in *Racine et la poésie tragique*, 1951, and *L'Action poétique dans le théâtre de Racine*, 1960.

misled by Romanticism into looking for one kind of poetry. Each will apply his own criteria and for my own part my admiration for the *Cid* does not extend to my thinking any part of it poetic. I find it an excellent play, classical in form and spirit, intelligent, fascinating. But at no point do the sentiments seem to suggest something beyond themselves, something of the order of what one can find on any page of La Fontaine. Where Corneille is poetic would seem to me to be in his envisaging of the tragic situation, in *Horace* the suggestions of demonic patriotism in the last Act (though their expression seems prosaic); in *Polyeucte* some of the lines seem so beautiful that they suggest more than a struck attitude, or a necessarily heroic gesture:

> Honteux attachements de la chair et du monde
> Que ne me quittez-vous, quand je vous ai quittés?

Or in a late play the courageous abandon of a general:

> Que tout meure avec moi, Madame. Que m'importe
> Qui foule après moi la terre qui me porte?
> Sentiront-ils percer, par un éclat nouveau,
> Ces illustres aieux, la nuit de leur tombeau?
> Respireront-ils l'air où les feront revivre
> Ces neveux qui peut-être auront peine à les suivre,
> Peut-être ne feront que les déshonorer,
> Et n'en auront le sang que pour dégénérer?
> Quand nous avons perdu le jour qui nous éclaire,
> Cette sorte de vie est bien imaginaire,
> Et le moindre moment d'un bonheur souhaité
> Vaut mieux qu'une si froide et vaine éternité.[1]

In such passages one feels (and it may be no more than an individual impression) that the description calls up

[1] *Suréna*, I. iii.

something more than the role or the *geste* required by the actor and the plot. How much more frequent is that feeling in Racine 'le plus humain des poètes'! The tragic moments in Racine seem to me much more naturally poetic than the dramatic moments in Corneille. I am not sure about 'Captive, toujours triste, importune à moi-même', or even 'J'ai mendié la mort chez des peuples cruels'; the appeal of both these may be that the line is so constructed not only to sound magnificent but to convey true poetry. But the suggestive power of the tragic figures communing with themselves at moments of insight may in Racine be most moving:

> Tu ne remportais pas une grande victoire,
> Perfide, en abusant ce cœur préoccupé,
> Qui lui-même craignait de se voir détrompé.

or

> Ah, qu'il eût mieux valu, plus sage et plus heureux,
> Et repoussant les traits d'un amour dangereux,
> Ne pas laisser remplir d'ardeurs empoisonnées
> Un cœur déjà glacé par le froid des années.

The cries of Phèdre are not individual cries: they are glimpses into humanity and its universal enigma. Is not this why one feels at any moment of that play that one is about to enter the realm of poetry? The suggestions of a struggle, within the creature, of man against God the Creator, is a theme that can only be called poetic. And is it not the constant suggestion of *Athalie*?

> Un songe (me devrais-je inquiéter d'un songe?)
> Entretient dans mon cœur un chagrin qui le ronge.
> Je l'évite partout, partout il me poursuit.

Perhaps these are only outcroppings, so to speak, of the poetry that animates Racinian tragedy, and that transcends any of the actual words and dramatic attitudes. The poetry discovered by the French classical dramatists is unjustly omitted from the anthologies, but one can see why. It resides in the conception of the tragic subject and not, as in Shakespeare, in its verbal expression. The subject of *Bajazet* is poetic; the symbolism of *Phèdre* and *Iphigénie* is poetic, and in a sense could we not say that there can be no more grandiose poetic subject than the war between creator and creature, that Racine has infused into the otherwise unedifying material of *Athalie*?

It is on these lines, I think, that the French think of Molière as a poet. Victor Hugo delighted in the verse of *L'Etourdi* and Boileau claimed to be lost in admiration of Molière's ability to find rhymes, but such features are not important in his work. It is not the lines or the images or the terms of *Le Misanthrope* that suggest poetry; in a sense Molière was working in a medium, that of realistic comedy, that precluded him from poetic flights. Where he is poetic, as Jouvet was never weary of insisting, is in his fantasy, that imagines and clothes with realism the boldest intellectual contrasts. This fantasy is as powerfully at work in the farces and the short plays as in the more reflective. The delightful fatuities of Jourdain, the naiveté and cowardice of Chrysale, do not annoy us or make us despise those characters; we enjoy them; their failings are a part of their humanity and the result is pleasure, for us for whom they were imagined. Some of the most daring flights of this gift of fancy are in plays that seem gross and elementary, such as *George Dandin*, where a man is made to look ridiculous time after time. But the idea behind this has nothing to do with an individual, clever or stupid, it is the persuasion common to all of us at times that our ideas and the way of the world are bound to clash. We would not mind, we say, suffering when we are in the wrong, but things go wrong when we are right. Alceste illustrates the point even more poetically than Dandin. Was it not also a bold and poetic fancy that imagined master and man in *Dom Juan*, a couple so neatly dovetailed into each other that the master could be shown as daring everything and the man as fearing anything? Such a contrast pleases by its form, and allows us to contemplate (without thinking we are engaged in an actual argument) the most risky views about the universe. Molière, in the full exercise of his profession as comedian, put on the stage, that is gave brief existence to, the most grotesque caricatures of humanity. The speed with which his figures flit across their stage is itself part of the poetry, at one moment lifelike, at the next absurd and unbelievable. One comes to feel that he can give poetic life to anything, for as long as we need to believe in it. 'C'est une imagination burlesque', as Toinette said in a moment of fanciful improvization.

III

THE
RENEWAL OF ROMANCE

It may seem perverse to include in an essay on French classicism a discussion of the novel. France produced no Cervantes, and Scarron may seem no match for Defoe. The important developments that have made of the novel the supreme modern literary kind take place in the eighteenth century and the one classical French novel that is still read would seem to be an exception.

But *La Princesse de Clèves* is not an isolated case. Its author owed much to her readers, and they read her as one among many, as an unusual example, perhaps, but not at all as a rarity or exception. Novels were for that aristocratic and middle-class public the most entertaining kind of reading matter, and they were read with much more attention than modern novels are read. In days when cheap editions and films did not exist, their only rival was the new drama, less satisfactory because it had to be enjoyed in public, at set times. Stories have been the delight of the cultured and the leisured in all periods of stable society. These romances were links in a long chain that includes Chrétien de Troyes, the *Amadis*, the *Astrée*, Rousseau, and George Sand. It is not impertinent to ask if the French writers who (we know) delighted in them did not undergo their influence.

Saintsbury was a great reader, but his dismissal of these stories has misled many people. He found them, understandably, dull and far too long, and concluded that they were formless, inartistic and unimportant. They are all these, now, to us who know what brevity and variety can do in the telling of stories. But their readers did not wish them to end, any more than readers of magazine serials wish them to end. To say that they were inartistic implies that they failed to reach a standard of form that we have since come to demand. The matter has been wrongly stated.

For Saintsbury, being one of the few people who gave time and patience to the reading of these many tomes, was too tired and exasperated by the effort to appreciate that they did not so much fail to achieve unity as dispense with it. In these hands, and for their type of reader, the novel was not an art form at all: it was an umbrella in which incidents held no more important place than discussions, questions, allegories. We should not say that the thread is easily lost, for the 'thread' was not the important thing to find. We should not say that we marvel how anyone could keep interest to the end, for probably no one did or tried to. They were read aloud, discussed, taken up and put down when the subject seemed attractive or to reach a pause. For Saintsbury the discussions got in the way; for La Fontaine they were part of the 'amusement', pastime, and as fascinating as the rest.

Here for example is a passage that probably proved as interesting and controversial as any incident: and as

controversial to contemporaries as it did later to
Ferdinand Brunot:

> Il s'agissait de savoir la force d'un mot dont on se sert
> ordinairement à table, et s'il faut dire: j'aime le fruit, j'aime le
> melon, je hais le sucre . . . Je fis valoir la beauté de la méta-
> phore et la force de l'usage autant que je le pus. . . . Elle
> voulut charitablement m'enseigner ce que c'était que le mot
> d'aimer, et la ridicule application qu'on en faisait à table à
> propos des fruits et des morceaux exquis qui peuvent estre
> objets de goût, mais non pas d'amour . . . Madame, de grâce,
> donnez-nous donc un mot qui vaille celui que vous nous
> ôtez. . . . Usez, dit-elle si vous voulez, du mot de goûter, du
> mot d'approuver. . . . Mais le mot d'aimer est infiniment au-
> dessus de cette basse expression que le peu de soin du bien
> dire laisse appliquer avec tant d'injustice et si peu de raison
> aux actions des sens et du goût.[2]

As soon as we grasp that the subject of these novels was
an imagined society, both like and unlike what their
readers knew, then we may put Fielding and Flaubert out
of our minds. To judge these novels by later fiction is to
assume that d'Urfé and his imitators were trying to do
what as yet they had no wish to do. We should think of
them rather as supplying entertainment, much in the manner of the modern magazine.

What was this entertainment? It included adventure,
turns of fortune, marvels, and disguises, but even more
discussion and conversation. Most of the conversation
dealt with standards (and this in itself might have shown
Saintsbury that he was on the wrong track), with conventions and concepts, with implications, particularly
social implications of what the individual thinks or plans

---

[2] Abbé de Pure, *La Prétieuse*, p. 196, apud F. Brunot, *Histoire de la
angue française*, III. i. 165.

or does or says. The constantly recurring assumption is that one cannot say or do what one likes . . . because of other people. The novels would not have been reprinted unless readers had liked to read of these cases, and demanded more. This means that they liked a form of literature that mirrored their own tastes, that allowed them to see their own social code in an ideal setting, where things like money or distance or class were no barrier. Truly, a world of escape.

M. Magendie, who more than any other scholar has revealed the secrets of these writings, makes the attractive suggestion that in jumping from point to point of social behaviour the novels displayed an early emergence of the classical spirit, by which he meant that spirit that is concerned to extract the general essence from a variety of cases. This may be so, but we should not think of it as consciously done. It is a by-product of an effort to amuse. Few things in that hard age allowed this type of escape from all-too-pressing realities. Is it any wonder that poets like Corneille and La Fontaine and Racine should find in these books the sort of world they sought?

The chief credit for inventing a world of fantasy into which readers might escape would seem to belong to Honoré d'Urfé. He alone showed the ability to construct a new type of fiction, to secure and maintain a large body of readers. (Here again, to speak of the unreality of the *Astrée* is to lose sight of what it set out to do.) He defends his elegant shepherds because their condition allowed description of a free and pleasant way of life:

vous n'avez toutes pris cette condition que pour vivre plus doucement et sans contrainte:

Like Boccaccio and Marguerite de Navarre he created

in this way a cadre of discussion, which was carried on by a small group of characters who soon became famous: Celadon the lover, Astrée the shepherdess, Hylas the independent, Sylvanire the socratic, Adamas the cleric. All these had adventures that ordinary people do not have; they spoke a language more elegant than everyday speech, telegraphic, witty, emblematic. Here one might read of a lovesick sceptic who spent six months in solitary (but apparently pleasant) retreat:

sur les bords de cette fontaine il bâtit une petite cabane, où il vécut retiré plus de six mois, durant lesquels sa plus ordinaire nourriture étaient les pleurs et les plaintes.

Such language was pleasing, even in hyperbole:

qu'elle sache que les nœuds dont je fus lié dès le commencement sont Gordiens, et que la mort seule en peut être l'Alexandre.

Yet the questions raised had often a homely directness:

Or celle-ci, dit Phyllis, est l'une des plus grandes folies du monde, les parents nous veulent choisir des maris, et nous sommes si sottes que nous les laissons faire.

Such a sentence was probably read by Molière, and almost certainly by Rousseau, and we know what resonance both of them were to give to the same point. According to the *Segraisiana*, the *Astrée* supplied material for the Paris stage for over forty years.

The entertainment given to a later generation by Gomberville, La Calprenède, Mme de Villedieu, and many others, does not seem different in kind. Practice may have made the writing less pretentious, but no less sententious; there would seem to be a touch of irony about the coincidences and the marvels. But Mlle de Scudéry would seem to have introduced a new interest. Her sketch of the dreamer, or absent-minded man, may be a pastiche of La Fontaine or Brancas; it is a clever pre-view of La Bruyère's Ménalque:

... certaine espèce de rêverie douce qui occupe et qui divertit l'esprit, et qui séduit quelquefois si doucement la raison qu'elle donne mille plaisirs qu'on ne saurait definir. Il est vrai, reprit Berelise, qu'il n'appartient pas à toutes sortes de gens de se mêler de rêver et qu'il y en a beaucoup qui en parlent qui ne savent pas ce que c'est que de laisser insensiblement égarer son esprit, en l'abandonnant plutôt aux mouvements de son cœur qu'à la conduite de cette impérieuse raison qui veut qu'on ne pense rien qu'elle n'ait approuvé. Car pour rêver doucement il faut laisser errer son esprit et le laisser aller sur sa foi; il faut être seul, il faut être aux champs, il faut avoir quelque chose dans l'âme qui ne déplaise pas, il faut être d'un tempérament un peu mélancholique, il faut vouloir ne penser à rien et penser pourtant à quelque chose, et ne penser pourtant à rien. Il faut être capable d'un certain endormissement des sens, qui fasse qu'on croie presque songer les choses à quoi l'on pense, et il faut enfin que l'usage de la raison soit suspendu jusqu'au point qu'on ne sache presque où l'on est. ...

Many such passages in Scudéry show an astonishing awareness of new social attitudes. She, with her skill for managing a drawing-room, had a sharp eye for the anti-social man. Her name for Alceste is Mégabate:

Mégabate, quoique d'un naturel fort violent est souverainement équitable. Comme Mégabate est fort juste, il est ennemi déclaré de la flatterie; il ne peut louer ce qu'il ne croit point digne de louange, et ne peut abaisser son âme à dire ce qu'il ne croit pas, aimant beaucoup mieux passer pour sévère auprès de ceux qui ne connaissent point la véritable vertu, que de s'exposer à passer pour flatteur. Aussi ne l'a-t-on jamais soupçonné de l'être de personne, et je suis persuadé que s'il eût été amoureux de quelque dame qui eût eu quelques légers défauts ou en sa beauté ou en son esprit, ou en son humeur, toute la violence de sa passion ne l'eût pu obliger à trahir ses sentiments. Ceux qui cherchent le plus à trouver à reprendre en lui ne l'accusent que de soutenir ses opinions avec trop de chaleur.

In the later volumes of the *Cyrus*, that is after the Fronde, Mlle de Scudéry practically converted what had been a fictional make-believe into a commentary on current events. This raised the novel at a stroke from a story into a sort of puzzle where the names were not hard to guess. Thus she writes of the Marquise de Rambouillet, of the Duchesse de Longueville, of Condé, and even describes his victories. This was to link the novel to the portrait and the memoir, inspired by the Fronde, and to the new fashion of judging behaviour that culminates in the social commentaries of Retz and Saint-Simon. Novels with this content were more than a pastime. They became a preacher's reading. Mascaron writes to the novelist:

L'occupation de mon automne est la lecture de *Cyrus*, de *Clélie* et d'*Ibrahim*. J'y trouve tant de choses propres à réformer le monde que je ne fais point de difficulté de vous avouer que, dans les sermons que je prépare pour la Cour, vous serez très souvent à côté de saint Augustin et de saint Bernard.

A similar thought seems to have occurred to Madame de Maintenon, who proposed to make the girls at Saint Cyr read the *Conversations* of Mlle de Scudéry.

If one now asks what sort of literature was spread and perfected by the novels, it would seem to be fiction with a difference. The externals are artificial but the situations seem close to reality. There is realism in the argument and artifice in the presentation. Was not the same tendency to be seen in the dramas of the time? Consider the general quoted from Corneille's play above (p. 44) or Pauline's words to Polyeucte, or Camille's outburst against state-worship. Such passages possibly imparted literary interest of a new kind. They were imagined, and thus not real enough to be taken into practical account. At the same time they touched on what was being thought and said about contemporary questions. This is surely a mark of classical literature and it is possible that it originated with the novels.

Novel readers in seventeenth-century France had, of course, other tastes. There were stories that seemed the reverse of idealistic or allegorical, stories that seemed to experiment with a much less artificial setting than the heroic novels. What share had Scarron and Furetière, and Sorel in the elaboration of a classical literature? I find this question admits of no clear answer. It is customary to think of literary production in France as running in two streams; realist and idealist are the usual terms. They mean little more than rough and polite. It would be pleasant to suggest that the two streams unite in classicism in which the heroics of Corneille and the elegance of Racine seem to parallel the realism of Molière and Boileau. But if one goes beneath surface impressions, it is difficult to see that *Le Roman Comique* or *Le Roman Bourgeois* either have classical features themselves or have inspired anything that might not have been written without them.

The one masterpiece of fiction created by a French classical author is much closer to the romanesque of d'Urfé and Scudéry than to any realistic tradition. The origin, and even the details of composition and of authorship of *La Princesse de Clèves*, are not known, but the work as we have it suggests that Mme de La Fayette (perhaps in conversation with La Rochefoucauld) discovered a way of presenting with more economy, and thus with greater effect, the study of love which she could find in many novels from the *Astrée* onwards. Thanks to the researches of Dr. Dallas we know that others had the same idea, and about the same time. Yet their efforts are forgotten and hers finds a place in modern discussions of the novel. She seems to have renewed a contemporary fashion and so limited her subjects as to give it a power which the restraint of her style makes memorable. And let us not forget, as historians of literature tend to do, that the power, even in the style, is imaginative power. It is the power of seeing a subject at a level where most people would not see it. This it is perhaps which accounts for the quality of French classical writing.

It is agreed that Mme de La Fayette composes her work in the way that is commonly called classical. This has been, one might say, proved by detailed comparison with her chief source, Brantôme.

Le mémorialiste écrit d'abondance, comme cela lui vient; il ignore l'art des gradations. Mme de La Fayette renverse à dessein l'ordre des idées: elle réserve pour la fin le portrait intellectuel et fait passer d'abord les données historiques. Et même là, elle s'attache à l'essentiel . . . cet art, à la fois subtil et savant, de condensation et de réduction, c'est l'art classique.[3]

Not only so but her work shows in a sharp light the

[3] H. Chamard & G. Rudler, 'Les Sources historiques de la Princesse de Clèves', *Revue du 16e siècle*, 1914, 1917.

limitations of vision of the seventeenth-century artist. Her work is a historical novel, based on a careful reading of actual texts. Yet it shows no sense of history, no appreciation either of the past or of individual qualities. She does not seem to wish to speak of differentiated individuals. Her characters are all perfect and stereotyped, very beautiful or very courteous or very brave. It is ironical that she should have found her theme in so vivid a writer as Brantôme, whose colours and sense of life she seems systematically to tone down: 'Elle voile, atténue, transpose, ennoblit, idéalise.' One wonders how the resulting story can have much life when she proceeds as she does. Even the vibrant figure of Nemours has become pale and perfectly courteous. 'Le brutal preneur de femmes du 16e siècle s'est mué en un Don Juan de cour, moins affiné de cœur que de manières.' He is described to us thus:

Ce prince était un chef d'œuvre de la nature. Ce qu'il avait de moins admirable c'était d'être l'homme du monde le mieux fait et le plus beau. Ce qui le mettait au-dessus des autres était une valeur incomparable, et un agrément dans son esprit, dans son visage et dans ses actions que l'on n'a jamais vu qu'à lui seul.

Here surely is the elegance of the classical manner, that in Racine makes Nero and Pyrrhus into polite courtiers, and that has seemed to later readers a proof of inability to portray things as they are.

Yet all this is done by design. Mme de La Fayette clearly does not want the life that is in the pages of Brantôme. She wants only his setting, and she intends within that setting to tell her story in her own way. It is a brilliant success and may transport us to a different world from that of the books that look so like hers, the *monde galant* of *Clélie* and *Cyrus*. These perfect people are in an impossible situation. In the long novels obstacles seemed to exist only to be overcome. Here the people are overcome by the obstacles, ironically, since they are almost by definition great and clever and almost perfect people. Their manners, even their good intentions, have almost no relevance in the tragic situation that ruins three lives. In a way the situation could not be further simplified: a high-principled girl marries a husband whom she respects and then meets a man she loves. It is as simple as that. Her life is poisoned (this is the word used) by the 'violent passion' that she must conceal. The precipice, the abyss (again these are the words) open before her as she is slowly destroyed by the absolute opposition between her duty and her inclination. As a seventeenth-century being, she is able to see both with unclouded eyes. This was only possible surely in that century. Before that, inclinations would not be deemed worthy to count. After that, the individual had learned of his 'sacred' right to get the most out of his life. When Rousseau handles this theme (his Julie is in similar plight) he so presents it that inclination seems right and social duty secondary. Not so the seventeenth-century heroine and authoress. In that still hierarchical age the loyalty promised to a husband is just as imperative as the violent passion of the lover. In this mature novel the incidents are arranged so as to bring out the force of the opposition. In themselves they are trivial: a meeting in a jeweller's, the theft of a portrait, a garden eavesdropping. Yet each seems to show more clearly than the previous one the 'abyss' that prevents happiness and any prospect of inner peace. As was once said of a masterpiece by Balzac: 'the incidents are trivial but the result is a broken life.'

With an irony reminiscent (to us) of Racine and La Fontaine the full force of the tragedy is brought home to the victim by the loving care of her husband. He refuses her requests to retire from the Court; he beseeches her to tell him the cause of her suffering. She forces herself to do so; it is the famous 'aveu', overheard as it happens by the eavesdropping lover. He lets out the secret and the two who thought they were alone find themselves suspecting each the other more than before. So honesty has proved the worst policy. The husband traps his wife by watching her when the suspected lover's name comes up: 'elle se trahit, comme Monime', as Rudler wrote. This only makes the position worse, and the story ends with unrelenting pressure, in the death of the husband, the retreat of the wife and the despair of the lover.

Such a theme would be depressing if not conveyed in a stylistic perspective that again makes one think of the technique of Racine. By accepting all the conventions of elegance, and by ruthless pruning of Renaissance detail, the ground is cleared, so to speak, for portrayal, at a distance, of an affective relationship. The vocabulary and style are worth study. It is the vocabulary of the emotions, not of things outside man, nor of events that happen to man. The reader may note the frequent recurrence of such words as calme, repos, trouble, aigreur, passion, embarras, agité, triste, malheureux. These words concern, not the things we do, so much as our intent or design in doing them; again the key words recur: aveu, persuasion, prédiction, prétexte, rigueur.

This bold abandon of traditional narration has enabled the artist to present a poetic theme with great power. Like a sort of seventeenth-century Jane Austen, she can generate situations of power, the more compelling because they are restrained, distanced, pitiless. The incidents, as said above, are few and ordinary. Not only so, they are symbolical: an accident on horseback, a dropped letter, a scarf trailing in the garden, these are impressive means of conveying apprehension, or the sense of incompatible forces behind human actions and words. It is not so much actual words that terrify the Princess as the sense of her own 'sensibilité' which for her is synonymous with lack of self-mastery: 'Ce lui était une grande douleur de voir qu'elle n'était plus maîtresse de cacher ses sentiments.' The famous *aveu*, over which contemporary readers argued, is not devastating in itself, but in the different reaction it evokes in a married couple. For the one it is the ultimate stage of confession; the other doubts whether it is the whole truth:

Vous n'avez pu me dire la vérité toute entière, vous m'avez caché la plus grande partie; vous vous êtes repentie même du peu que vous m'avez avoué et vous n'avez pas eu la force de continuer. Je suis plus malheureux que je ne l'ai cru et je suis le plus malheureux de tous les hommes.

Not only the presentation but the content seems to be Racinian. This design of portraying duty and inclination, at maximum tension and in conflict, is a main feature of *Phèdre*. The play was probably planned a year or two later than the novel. Phèdre is in the grip of a natural passion; her marriage obligation prevents her from yielding to that which her whole being desires, and she is destroyed in the process. Racine envisages jealousy and crime as part of this tragic condition. Mme de Clèves feels jealousy but admits to no crime. Yet it is the same tragic condition. Thus classical tragedy and the classical novel explore the same mystery, from different angles. The one probes the coexistence of passion and conscience; the other, hardly less profoundly, the coexistence of passion and the marriage bond. For all her classical reticence is not Mme de La Fayette's verdict as damning as that of Goethe and Rousseau?

If one were to pursue this line of thought, would not French classical art appear to involve a sort of dialogue on the tragic implications of the fact of humanity? If the fact of being human involves these irreconcilables, then only an art compounded of reticence and imagination could attempt to suggest them. And do not Molière, Pascal, La Fontaine all envisage something similar: the features of humanity, usually the warring and opposing features? Never before, and never since, could a modern society contemplate with vigour and equanimity so vast and deep a picture. Classicism was perhaps a precarious moment of vision.

IV

THE
RECOVERY OF TRAGEDY

'LE passé littéraire c'est quelques livres qui subsistent.'
The point seems obvious when put so clearly, but it needs
a critic as acute as Thibaudet for its adequate formulation.
To read some textbooks one would think that the entire
dramatic production of the century in France was in
preparation for, or in consequence of, the genius of
Corneille and Racine. Yet, as scholars have proved, the
works of these two dramatists, and of those who
agreed with or who copied them, are a tiny proportion
of the plays produced and acted in France in their day.
Mornet's new *History*, using Lancaster's exhaustive
survey, estimates nearly four hundred plays produced
between 1660 and 1690. Most of these were soon forgotten; a few attracted increasing attention. What was it
in them that drew audiences, that compelled comment,
that enraged rivals, and that to later writers has seemed
so essentially 'French', so 'classical'?

The greatness of the few is discernible if we look carefully at the mass. To continue with Thibaudet: 'Les

œuvres du passé ne sauraient être comprises et jugées que par ceux qui savent le passé.' Time after time, in plays now forgotten, one finds attempts and approaches at what is perfectly done by Corneille. The interest, for example, is not (as it was in many plays of the early century) in the story, the events. The public seems to have preferred plays about a situation, about attitudes and motives, about choices and decisions. It is not only in Corneille that reflection seems to replace action, that the point seems to be not so much in what people do, as in their attitude to what is done. In this sense *Le Cid* is typical: 'Je sais ce que je suis et ce que je dois faire', . . . 'Je le ferais encore si j'avais à le faire'.

There were many causes for this. It was partly due to Senecan influence, partly also to the tradition of rhetoric in the schools. It would seem likely to make the plays less dramatic, but this is offset by a remarkable vigour of treatment, an improvement in dramatic technique which again seems to have been due to no single author but, no doubt, to the pressures of public performance. Reflections are not pointless but calculated, and opposed, in scenes that aim at a pattern. The scholar who has been into the evidence most carefully claims that this type of play is an invention of French seventeenth-century culture:

La conception de la dramaturgie au 17e siècle apporte en effet une série d'innovations dont il n'est pas exagéré de dire qu'elles créent le théâtre moderne. Les apparitions du héros dans la pièce sont calculées et exploitées au maximum; les obstacles ne sont plus des idées ou des fatalités, mais deviennent des personnages vivants, liés les uns aux autres par un indéchirable réseau de sentiments.[4]

What therefore these dramatists seem to take away with

[4] J. Schérer, *La Dramaturgie classique en France*, p. 434.

one hand, by cutting out much of what we might call action, they give back with the other, by restricting the number of characters and arranging their carefully-linked appearances. They seem to aim at creating an illusion of action round a single event involving strong feelings, and to concentrate on making this more effective than any recreation of events could be. This is what people mean who say that French classical drama allows of no development in character or plot, that it takes an event at the moment of crisis. The fact has been frequently noticed, but not so often the enormous increase in dramatic suspense that it permitted. No wonder, surely, that dramatists with such aims should welcome the new dramatic theories worked out in Italy, known as the unities. By discouraging changes of time and place and diversity of interest these could be powerful aids to concentration. It is absurd to think that the unities were adopted because authors were persuaded to write according to rule, and that (as Victor Hugo suggested) a 'free' Corneille would have produced finer plays. It is reasonable to assume that skilled playwrights adopted such 'rules' only because they allowed greater suspense and concentration than any sequence of events would have done.

There is no better proof of all this than *Le Cid*. Over-praised as the first classical play, which is unfair to Mairet and Rotrou and Tristan, all of whom wrote 'regular' plays about the same time, the play is a beautiful example of how dramatic interest is increased by concentration of the material. Its Spanish source is divided into three 'days' of events, of which Corneille leaves out as much as he adopts. His first Act contains nothing that does not concern the emotional situation of Rodrigue. The first day of the Spanish play has several changes of scene, a duel, a riot, a lament, an appeal of the injured courtier to his three sons for vengeance. Corneille did not invent this type of drama. To be historically just we should remember that his gifted contemporaries experimented with it even before he did. But popular taste, then and since, has singled him out and neglected the others, and understandably so, for his dramatic versatility was extraordinary. For over forty years he produced plays in which the main character was forced to decisions, placed in dilemmas, confronted with problems.

In a sense his task was made more difficult by the standard of merit set by his own early plays, as also by the fact that he was not free, as writers of comedy were, to invent plots. Serious drama must have the support of history. All his tragedies are therefore historical and presuppose an enormous amount of reading. For this immense industry and its dramatic application he received the admiration of his contemporaries—did not Voltaire say he had been called 'le grand Corneille' to distinguish him not from his brother, but from all other men?—but from his modern critics hardly any credit. Yet the man who could treat so many subjects, please so many people, write so many lines, so many of them dramatic, win the admiration of the pit no less than that of Dryden, such a man must be reckoned distinguished in his art. He surely did more than any other single writer to establish what was in fact a new form of dramatic art; without his work that of Racine is unthinkable. 'Avant lui la tragédie classique n'existait pas. Par lui elle a existé.'[5]

The phrase brings us to the real subject of this chapter. For it is one thing to recognize Corneille as an industrious and inventive dramatist, and quite another to say that he

[5] G. Lanson, *Pierre Corneille*, 1898, p. 187.

created classical tragedy. He was chiefly concerned to manufacture the serious play, that should affect the feelings of the spectators. When in defending his work against a new generation he tried to explain what he had created, he found great difficulty in fitting it to the Aristotelian categories. He seems in fact to have stumbled upon tragedy, as it were accidentally, in the course of working out the serious play. *Le Cid* was neither written as a tragedy, nor at first so called. Its description was changed from 'tragi-comédie' to 'tragédie' because its theme and form suggested the tension, and had on the public the effect, of tragedy. Voltaire explained this by saying that 'Avant *le Cid* on ne connaissait point encore ce combat des passions qui déchire le cœur et devant lequel toutes les beautés de l'art ne sont que des beautés inanimées.'

If we press this point and ask what the contemporaries of Corneille and Racine thought tragedy was, the answer is not easy to find. Neither poet wrote much on dramatic theory. The prefaces of Racine, like the Discourses of Corneille, were an answer to critics. Corneille said that a tragedy was held together by unity of peril. The working out of that peril to what we call a happy ending did not seem to matter. Neither he nor Racine thought that tragedies need end in death. He doubted the Aristotelian explanation of a catharsis. Racine defined the pleasure of tragedy as a feeling of dignity and pity (or melancholy) aroused by the whole work: 'que tout se ressente de cette tristesse majestueuse qui fait tout le plaisir de la tragédie.' The practice of these two artists is more interesting than their views. Had Corneille, as some think, no real sense of tragedy? Are not his plays dramatic rather than tragic? Is not French classical tragedy, in the strict sense of the word, written by Racine alone? These questions have never, to my mind, been satisfactorily answered.

Most readers would agree that the greater part of Corneille's dramas convey no true sense of tragedy. They have their tragic moments, such as Rodrigue and Chimene seeing no end to their unhappiness, Cléopâtre about to poison Rodogune, Sertorius defying tradition ('Rome n'est plus dans Rome, elle est toute où je suis'). These and similar passages suggest acutely dramatic moments, often with tragic implications. This poet excels in opposing people to events or to each other. Tragic outcome, such as death, disaster, sacrifice, despair, is infrequent. Only in one brief period of his career, in the five years after *Le Cid*, when he seemed conscious of his new powers and before he was pressed to produce a stream of sensational plays, does he seem to have come upon (rather than sought) true tragedy. *Cinna* seems to me a tense play, and a strong play, in which the conflicts are resolved. *Polyeucte* on the other hand would seem rightly called a tragedy, since conflicts are therein suggested that are not resolved. This is not because it is about martyrdom. Death for the martyr is sweet, and sought; it means for him triumph, and not defeat:

Je consens, ou plutôt j'aspire, à ma ruine.

Yet through this drama of indecision and argument there runs a sense of the tragedy of fanaticism. Polyeucte, though not tragic as a martyr, seems to me so as a fanatic. The fanatic sees one thing only; in the play he is brought up against another, a conflicting affection. His marriage is a disaster, since he is a man who wishes to stake everything on a single aim and on undivided loyalty. He therefore tries to deny that any conflicting claim exists:

'Je ne vous connais plus si vous n'êtes chrétienne.' In almost the same words Horace had denied that the family can come before the state: 'Albe vous a nommé, je ne vous connais plus.'

As the play proceeds this contrast becomes much more than one of individuals or of preferences. It takes on tragic and universal proportions. The poet suggests the unbridgeable gulf that separates the church from the world. For the former, no claim can interfere with the divine command; for the latter, society and nature must also be heard. Each is bound to think the other mistaken. What to the one appear as 'célestes vérités', to the other are figments, 'imaginations'. Where the believer sees 'éternelles clartés', the world sees only an 'étrange aveuglement'. Corneille did not invent this tragic split: he discerned it and made it the culmination of his dramatic argument. But it was deep in French life and he could see evidence of it no doubt all round him: in the Jansenists, two of whom converted Pascal in Corneille's own town about the time of this play. Still more in the Protestants, for whom the choice of family or faith was real and agonising. Tallemant tells of one Huguenot fanatic whose wife had to be protected against him because he threatened to sacrifice her as the biblical patriarch had been ready to sacrifice his son, in order that submission to God's command be made clear.

Fanaticism indeed seems to have been the one theme that provoked Corneille to go beyond the merely theatrical. The death of Suréna (a sort of Wallenstein) and even the desperate Senecan violence of Medea, have lost any tragic force that they may have had. *Horace* seems to me to be Corneille's only real tragedy. The conflict of the Roman champions against three Albans linked to their family gives him a fine dramatic situation, which if exploited as a story, as he found it in Livy, would have been extraordinary and unreal, but which served him for admirable opposition of types in war. The humanity of Curiace is the appropriate foil to the fire-eating patriotism of Horace, whose sister shows in her pacifism the same uncompromising fanatical strain that animates her brother as a warrior. The full tragic implications of this opposition are made clear after the murder. The fifth Act, which some find dull and which André Gide thought admirable, commits the decision to a court, and to the audience. Is the man to be acclaimed as the saviour of the state, or executed as a murderer? For he is both, and not by chance, but by virtue of his chief quality.

This quality might be called demonic heroism. It is demonic because it produces both glory and shame. To save the state in battle calls for fanatical qualities, scorn of compromise, rejection of all considerations save one: that the state is right and demands entire allegiance. Polyeucte, as we saw, thinks much the same as this about religion. But to deal with a fractious relative, a conflict of view within a family, calls for other qualities, tolerance, humanity, the broad view, for just those qualities in fact which the out-and-out soldier does not and cannot possess. This is surely more than just theatre. It shows how in Corneille's hands a play can make concepts and contrasts as living as what we like to call 'real people'. And it may be called tragic, for it suggests a conflict of incompatible and irreconcilable qualities: 'Il n'y a pas d'héroisme patriotique sans terrorisme chauvin.'[6]
Apart from this admittedly intellectual type of tragedy,

[6] Vedel, *Deux classiques français*, 1935, p. 96.

I do not think that a case can be made out for Corneille as a tragic poet. In his work France recovered, not tragedy itself so much as a vehicle for tragedy: the tragic style, the tragic tension, the concentration on a situation at once impenetrable and unavoidable. To illustrate this new dramatic power in play after play was to create a marvellous instrument. Is it not one of the great accidents of art history (for I see no adequate explanation) that among the first to use the instrument should be one of the world's greatest tragic poets?

Everything about Racine is unusual. His tragedies were nearly all produced within a decade, before he was forty, and in circumstances which for most men would have been disturbing and distracting. Yet at least seven times in that decade he created a dramatic spectacle so impressive that it has been played and studied for nearly three hundred years, and with increasing respect. It is, to say the least, an achievement as notable as that of Corneille in the 1640s and of Molière in the 1660s, and alongside theirs it suggests an immense reserve of intellectual and artistic energy in the French middle class of that age. It is in fact these seven plays that enable us to speak of a recovery of tragedy, the only French achievement comparable to the great age of the Athenian or the Elizabethan drama. We may assume that audiences of Racine experienced something comparable to audiences of *Oedipus* and of *Othello*, the full paradoxical power of tragic action, exalting and impressive where it was most annihilating and inscrutable.

No manuscripts survive, but the sources and structure of each of these plays have been studied, and it should be possible for us to discern at least the main features of what the poet had in mind. So regarded the plays appear as a series of daring dramatic experiments, attempts to read into a chosen historical situation a conflict of forces that transcend that situation, a picture of the tragic human condition. This picture was in each case only obtained at a cost; the structure fabricated scene by scene does not completely convey the idea, and the illusion is not everywhere convincing. Students who feel this should not be told that it is impious to criticise great art, but should be encouraged to see the vision which the poet seems to have tried to create. For Racine, as for Gautier, and for the sculptor whom Gautier had in mind, the intention had somehow to be transferred to 'matière rebelle'. In admiring the structure let us not forget that the rarest poetic insights are not perfectly communicable; they may occur in a play where the cohesion or the illusion is not fully convincing.

It is arguable that Racine constructed his best dramatic machine in *Andromaque*, that never again did he find an issue of such pathetic force, linking four characters so closely that any move by any one of them would affect them all. The ingenuity of this machinery at times helps, and at other times hinders, the communication of tragedy. If Oreste is to depend on Hermione, she on Pyrrhus, he on Andromaque and she on her son, the whole action hinges on the credibility of her yielding to Pyrrhus with the secret design of killing herself at the altar. We may feel that this is not likely to save Astyanax, but it does allow each character to hope for the impossible: Andromaque for freedom from Pyrrhus, Pyrrhus for union with Andromaque, Hermione for Pyrrhus and Oreste for Hermione.

In all drama the spectator surveys the whole field, most of which is hidden from each character, but Racine's skill in this play is to use this double vision to suggest the tragic irony of all human action. As M. Picard has written: 'L'action tragique est cette action catastrophique que le personnage poursuit parce qu'il le croit efficace, mais que le spectateur sait illusoire ou ironiquement et désastreusement efficace.' The very helplessness of these figures excites pity even when they scorn and blame each other. The furious woman who whips her lover for inconstancy: 'Tout cela part d'un cœur toujours maître de soi' is the last person who should speak so; she is terrified by her own inconstancy: 'Je crains de me connaître en l'état où je suis'. The ultimate victim of all this, Oreste, in a final demonic vision of his failing reason, sees serpents round his head and all things returning to obscurity: 'Venez-vous m'enlever dans l'éternelle nuit?'. It is curious that so tense a drama should convey such poetry, but it may be significant that its chief source was Virgil and that the verse, no less than the structure, conveys the tragedy. In Racine, says Maulnier, there are no heroes, there are only victims, and these victims hardly need names. Their qualities animate them: we see them as 'captive' or as 'inconstant' or as 'aveugle' or as 'une amante en furie'. This is new, in dramatic history, and yet very old. Is it not a return to medieval and ancient categories, but with a precision of technique and a music of verse that can convey through those categories a modern vision?

In *Britannicus* we may watch this brilliant technique at work on an apparently historical case, again involving three or four interlocked relationships, again suggesting decisions of life and death, taken by people incapable of real decision, because they are master neither of the situation nor of themselves. The choice of the death of

Britannicus as the tragic subject is a perfect occasion for the poet to explore a first break in the dependence of Nero upon his mother. This is the central issue of the play and is conveyed with greater poetic range than even Tacitus could give to it. Again, we watch the victims, Britannicus and Junie, dependent on the cruelty of Nero, the exercise of which is dependent on the exasperation caused by Agrippine. So these victims are the victims of victims. Decisions are inevitable. Yet nowhere are the decisions taken with responsibility, integrity, real moral command of a situation. They are occasioned, they are ways out of an intolerable relationship. The play has been called an 'astonishing apology for Nero' and certainly this is not the Nero of history. But neither does it claim to be a rewriting of history, to be set (as M. Lanson set it) beside the Nero of Renan. The poet does not interpret; he imagines, not a historical character but a possible historical situation in which influences good and bad can be arranged to play upon a central figure, who has all power, but no power of decision, no principles, only instincts and impulses. It is a delicate balance, that might swing either way. The Emperor is swayed by Burrhus for good as he is by Narcisse for evil. The force that upsets this balance, that ensures unwittingly but catastrophically the triumph of evil, is the mother. As we watch her restless plotting and desire for lost power we feel that any course of action imposed by her would lose its moral force: it would not be a free choice. So tightly is this net drawn that Nero has no way to independent action but the wrong way: he cannot attain freedom except by crime. Between him and a choice of good stands his feared and fearsome mother. This pitiless play (which Giraudoux compared to *Wuthering Heights*) seems less imposing in its vision of tragic humanity than *Andromaque*, but this impression fades as we grasp the ironic power with which the poet shows us the start of a criminal career without any strong volition to be a criminal. The mystery that surrounds 'decision', the connection between weakness and wickedness, has rarely been suggested with such force.

The author of these two tragedies showed unusual skill in the selection of a theme containing possibilities both dramatic and poetic. It is not surprising therefore to find him attempting a dramatic treatment of the single sentence 'Titus Berenicen ab urbe dimisit invitus invitam'. He delights in showing the balance of forces that could here be envisaged: the state interests that prevent lovers from uniting, the love which prevents happiness except together. The historical situation clearly seized and brought as it were to its point of ultimate simplification is treated as a case of mortals desiring a happiness which in the nature of things they cannot attain. At this point the issue ceases to be of historical interest, it becomes a picture of the human condition. 'Bérénice has nothing to do with Palestine, and it is impossible to care whether she is a queen or not. She does not inhabit that mortal realm in which racial tradition, geography, social status and the historical context have their fatal importance. Because Racine is interested in only one moment of psychic life, he replaces all the rest with purely illustrative conventional signs.'[7] The simplicity and force of the feelings portrayed in this play are put into strong relief by one of the most remarkable Racinian experiments: the omission of the conventional tragic ending. Since for these characters separation is complete tragedy, since their

[7] F. Ferguson, *Idea of a Theater*, 1956, p. 56.

happiness consists only in their being together, death would not complete their tragedy. 'Il n'est pas nécessaire qu'il y ait du sang et des morts dans une tragédie.' So firmly has this poet recovered the notion of the tragic that he can present a tragedy without death.

In *Bajazet* (1672) he makes yet another break with tradition, by taking a contemporary subject from an oral source, a tale told by the Turkish ambassador. The situation and the characters are of a kind that would appeal to the creator of Hermione. The sultane herself is little more than a slave, under sentence of death, who in her lord's absence requires a prince to marry her, or die. Since he is prepared to die, her desolation is complete; her happiness is in him; her threat of force is without effect; she knows no other weapons. The marvel is how a situation so simplified could fill five Acts of a tragedy. The local colour is brilliantly used, but every scene advances the theme; once again it is the tragedy of 'no escape'. But (and after *Bérénice* this should not surprise) the tragic outcome is not death, though every character is done to death. The tragic figure is not Bajazet, but Roxane, who has power over him, uses it to the full and to her own misery. It is the tragedy of Hermione but on a more impressive scale, raised now to the central theme of the drama. It is almost the tragedy of the absurd: life lived on Roxane's terms is meaningless. Her only weapons are physical and they are out of place in a world of persons.

One scholar sees this play as a clinical exploration into the domain of primitive feeling:

Le sentiment qui anime Bajazet, Atalide, Roxane, sous un art accompli, déguise à peine l'instinct. Il suit son chemin en des âmes primitives où rien ne l'arrête et il parvient tout naturellement à son terme qui dans la circonstance est la mort.[8]

This may be so. Yet I think the primitive is part of the poetic suggestion rather than of the exploration of human nature. Is Roxane any more primitive than Hermione, or Néron? Are not all these plays attempts to imagine the ultimate effects of *amour-propre*, that devouring egoism and pride which La Rochefoucauld described in terms that fit the Racinian drama? Racine's pictures of this pride are not repetitive but they are similar. His method seems to seek a situation where force may be confronted by dignity, and where the physical overpowering of the defenceless is not the sole or even the dominant feature of the encounter.

Mithridate (1673) enforces this impression. It is said to have been the favourite play of Louis XIV, and one can see why. This spectacular king, restless and violent, feared at home and abroad, the implacable enemy of Rome, no sooner beaten than planning another attack on the eternal enemy, has enough dramatic energy to fill a play. Yet his chief enemy, his victor, is not Rome but a girl, who brings home to him, much as Bajazet tried to persuade Roxane, that power and fraud may win battles, but cannot win respect. It has been suggested that in both these plays things are so arranged that a violent figure is forced to enter, or to admit, a moral universe. 'In *Bajazet* as in *Mithridate* the central figure embarks on a campaign of discovery.'[9]

The poet certainly makes the most of the sentimental situation he has thus repeatedly imagined. It must have been of great effect in his time, and on his stage. In a theatre where physical action is banned, those who rely on it are the more easily shown as the victims or as

[8] G. Truc, *Jean Racine*, 1926, p. 98.
[9] J. C. Lapp, *Aspects of Racinian Tragedy*, 1955, p. 142.

morally defeated by their victims. But more than an appealing spectacle is involved. To use the powerless to rebuke the powerful is not only a theatrical effect; it is a means of suggesting a poet's judgement on human forces. It allows him to develop a kind of tragedy that perhaps no other poet has attempted. To define this we should have to note the alliance of two features not often found in company. The one is a pitiless judgement on human behaviour; the other is a clear view of what constitutes moral strength and weakness. In these plays suffering comes with apparent indifference on both innocent and guilty, but there is a difference: the former are unfortunate, the latter are unhappy. Violence seems to thwart the one who employs it. In each play there seems to be some figure who lacks self-mastery and who is made the architect of his or her own misery. This is a feature that requires exploration and analysis; we should not assume it is a result of the poet's Christian training; it might well be a Stoic conception. The impressive thing, as one reads the tragedies, is the constant poetic sugges-tion of the nature and limits of humanity: inhuman things are done by people who are (in and after doing them) all-too-human, who are weak when they seem strong, who are afraid when they protest assurance:

> Je ne le croirai point? Vain espoir qui me flatte,
> Tu ne le crois que trop, malheureux Mithridate.

Is it an accident that these unforgettable pictures of the tragic implications of humanity should have been imagined in Paris during the very years that Molière was imagining equally impressive comic pictures of the limits of the human condition? Or might we see in French classical comedy and tragedy a single principle at work?

The last two public tragedies of Racine suggest that he wished still further to explore the range of tragedy. Both *Iphigénie* (1674) and *Phèdre* (1677) contain a new emphasis on the supernatural. So far men have contended with men, in these two plays they contend with gods. One can imagine a student of Greek drama, as Racine was, concerned with the possibility of recovering this area of experience for modern tragedy. He seems to have attempted it through style. The images become more fluid, ambiguous, mysterious, symbolical. A case in point is the word *autel*, of which Mr. Lapp has counted thirty-nine cases in *Iphigénie*, a play in which one would expect it to recur, but not with the suggestions of both its meanings, as a place of marriage vows and of sacrifice. *Phèdre* too is a play about gods and men. Just as in Euripides Artemis and Aphrodite presided over human action, so here Racine uses Venus and Neptune, and the elements of nature which symbolise their power, to suggest infinite extension of what reason knows as nature. In this play the sun, and the light of day, are divine. Minos suggests mysterious regions which seem to be both Christian and pagan. Events happen on two planes: the human scene is never, as in Racine's previous plays always, the whole of the picture. Were it not again for the superb style, the tragic impression would be blurred rather than fused. But by this fusion the poet conveys a sense of inscrutable mystery for which the ancient legend of Phaedra seems the entirely fitting vehicle.[1]

[1] I see that I have said nothing of the theological undertones of this play. Leo Spitzer (*Linguistics and Literary History*, 1948) interprets it as a tragedy of *desengaño*, in which we are asked to contemplate the condition of men under the inexorable and unjust rule of the gods. Although I do not find his argument convincing, the play does seem to present the human condition as in itself tragic, particularly in its vision of instinct at war with conscience.

This amazing play is as full of intellectual content as it is of myth and mystery. The scholar who seems to have studied the poet most closely calls it 'une tragédie mythologique, traversée par une réflexion rationaliste'. In uniting myth and modern reflexion Racine reached this ultimate achievement in the recovery of tragedy. He referred to it in his preface as 'the most reasonable' of his works, by which perhaps we should understand that he felt it to correspond most nearly to the facts of the human condition. Of all his works, this was the one in which the process of art had illumined rather than falsified the suggestion of humanity. But who may say with confidence what was in a poet's mind?

This astounding poetic career was to remain unexpected to the end. There is a postscript to his plays, written twenty years later in the form of two biblical dramas for Mme de Maintenon. French scholars like to savour this paradox: 'le plus sensuel et le plus terrible des poètes écrit des tragédies pour des petites filles.' Yet these subjects from the Old Testament seem suited to what we know of his poetic preference. They gave him the pitiless and brutal element that he seems to have sought in any tragic subject. They allowed him to portray life as conflict, not only of man against man, and of man against divine powers, but of man against the One God. *Athalie*, as already suggested, seems thus to figure the most dramatic and basic of all conflicts, that of the creature against the creator. As Milton with Satan, so Racine opposes his impious queen not only to the priests but to her own conscience. For her the God of the Hebrews is an enemy and an equal, who attacks her in dream and in solitude as well as in the open:

'. . . Vingt fois en un jour à moi-même opposée.' We

may feel with Voltaire that this *tour de force* has upset the dramatic intention, that the evocation of this magnificent figure of revolt has meant that by contrast official religion appears as harsh and inhuman: '*Athalie* qui est le chef-d'œuvre de la belle poésie n'en est pas moins le chef-d'œuvre du fanatisme.' So there is paradox to the end. Such was the legacy of an orthodox poet to a century of irreligion.

V

THE

DISCOVERY OF COMEDY

We may properly say that Racine recovered tragedy in a pure form for the modern world. But we ought not in the same way to say that Molière recovered comedy, even though he gave his audiences something that Europeans had not enjoyed perhaps since Plautus. Looked at in the large his work is not recovery of an ancient art so much as discovery of a new one. 'Molière a tiré la comédie du chaos,' said Voltaire, thinking no doubt of the mediocrity of his predecessors. This would seem unjust to the pioneer work, as it now appears, of Rotrou and Scarron and Desmarets. But Voltaire probably meant, not that Molière wrote better than others, but that he offered a kind of comedy beside which all other types seemed muddled and elementary. This possibility has never, I think, been taken seriously outside Moliere's own country. How should one define his creation? What sort of thing is it that goes by the name of classical comedy?

The world, said Sir Thomas Browne, took six days to make, and is like to take six thousand years to make out.

We might say of the greatest of French writers that he made, in fourteen years, what it may take over four hundred years to make out. His work has so far resisted all attempts at neat explanation. To see it as a reflection of his life, or of his ideas, has led to nothing, for we know little of his real life, as of his ideas, and the type of play that he had to produce is a poor vehicle for either. The main fact that we do know is that he lived for the theatre. There is no guide to the interpretation of his works, other than the theatrical conditions in which he made them. These have been investigated: the tradition in which he acted, the actors that he gathered and trained, the sort of audience that made his reputation in the hall of the Palais Royal, near the present site of the Comédie Française. We know that there, for twelve years, he worked for his audience and his company, a triple activity of manager, author and actor, that caused him to die exhausted at fifty-one. Such a life left little scope for making the theatre into a pulpit and there is no evidence that he wished it to become such. Let us be satisfied with what we know, that the financial fortunes of his company were a constant problem, that therefore the plays had to be written at speed, with an eye to popular success, and that to air doctrine or to indulge in satire, otherwise than incidentally, would have been disastrous. This is almost the limit of our knowledge, other conclusions about this comedy are conjectural, possible but unverifiable: it must be interpreted as theatre if it is to be interpreted at all. A beginning has been made, but it is possible to study, much more rigorously than we have yet done, the sort of pleasure that Molière supplied, the sort of satisfaction which, after all, was what caused the plays to be printed, translated and endlessly repeated on stage.

As it happens we do have the source of his first long verse comedy, the *Ecole des Femmes*, performed on December 26, 1662. We may thus put side by side the rough material that seems to have given him his idea, and the finished product that was played thirty-four times, brought in nearly 30,000 livres and started a noisy literary quarrel. Surely here minute comparison may give us some hint of what precisely it is that is novel and dynamic in a play that Thibaudet seemed to consider the most comic of all. The source is a silly story, of a man who thought clever wives were bound to be unfaithful and so decided to marry a fool. Not only so but to train her shielding her from modern ideas and dangerous knowledge. He lectured her on marriage and made her keep guard over him while he slept, and of course lost her to a passing gallant.

In this tall story did Molière find the theme of his first masterpiece. It is fairly clear how he dealt with it. He neglected the obvious absurdities and enforced the main idea, which gave him room to play about with a comic issue of some subtlety: a man playing for safety by taking a fool for a wife. But only a fool would take a fool. Who is then the fool? There are possibilities here, on a clear basis such as the theatre needs. The more methodical a fool can be, the more sense and brain he can put into his folly, the sharper the delight at seeing his plan unfold and come to ruin. This was to modernise a very old French tradition, of the pedant, the doctor in the farce. It is basic in Molière as in most comic literature. But he found more in Scarron's tale; he found the suggestion of a figure that opposed the fool at all points, the artless girl made stupid, trained to be a tool. It is Molière, not Scarron, who saw that the poetic counterpart, almost the logical and esthetic double, of the pedant is the ingénue, without education she has only nature to rely on, an attractive spectacle for a sophisticated audience. What has happened? It is as if the tall story had passed through an artist's brain, discerning, omitting, fusing, elements that suggest (and perhaps do no more than suggest) deep comic antagonisms. A war between education and nature is at the least a wide theme. But the artist is not satisfied to leave the problem so. That would oppose a natural girl to an unnatural pedant. But nature is in all of us, can it not be shown in Arnolphe? So, again leaving Scarron far behind, a third and most intriguing contrast is suggested. The pedantry is not the whole man. The pedant is susceptible, to the charms of his stultified ward. He cannot resist the attraction of a being whom he has striven to make unattractive.

Thus the characters are traditional: pedant, ingénue, gallant. They are recognizable, whether they actually wore the mask or not. The mask stamps the character for the audience; as Mascarille Molière wore it (or a little mask?) and later discarded it. But that was the tradition in which he was working. Yet these well-worn characters are opposed and moved around with an easy and intelligent mastery that allows of both realism (of gesture) and poetry (of symbolic suggestion). There is no need of comic reversals of fortune. They are used, at the end of this play, but they are no longer the comic attraction. The new reversals are not incidents, but attitudes, developing with comic disproportion and surprise: the School for Wives, by an expert who thought he knew it all, and who bragged of his confidence and dictated his orders, and was defeated by untutored human nature, that showed him he had not even mastered the elements and reduced him from a tyrannical professional to stammering flirtation. Are we to say that the comedian who could imagine and stage these things was not a new kind of comic poet?

The novelty, however, is elusive to those seeking to define. It is not in the subject: men made plays in the middle ages about all Molière's subjects. It is not at first sight in the content of ideas. The theologian was almost certainly wrong who thought *Le Bourgeois Gentilhomme* a plea for the old order. The subjects of the comedies are indeed dangerous: it is understandable that *Tartuffe* and *Dom Juan* were banned in 1664 and 1665. But they were banned for what they were about, rather than for actual subversive views. The novelty lay perhaps in the suggestiveness of the attitudes; in the case of *Dom Juan* this would mean not any views on atheism so much as the opposition of hedonism and superstition; in the case of *Tartuffe* we might find it in the almost insolent coupling of mock piety and sensuality. The background of these inventive associations has not been discovered; for the moment let us note that they account for much of the drama and the comedy, and that they occur with most brilliance in the slight plays. As in painting the sketch or caricature has an effect which the oil painting has not, so Diderot said it must have taken as much genius to write *Pourceaugnac* as *Tartuffe*. The comedy of fatuity is easier to grasp than the comedy of duplicity but that does not say it was easier to create.

Such a play as *Le Médecin malgré lui* is not supposed to have any structure worth studying. Yet one cannot think that its great success was due to a series of happy inspirations that allowed scenes to be strung together in loose (and lucky) sequence. To a graduate class in California that attempted analysis of the comic material, this play disclosed some interesting forms and features. In the central Act of three the main scene is a mock consultation by the bogus doctor who is really a woodcutter. This is balanced by a main scene in the third Act showing (like the old tale) the doctor curing a dumb girl, and by a main scene in the first Act showing how a family quarrel and a wife's natural desire for revenge made her say that her husband would admit to being a doctor if he were beaten hard enough. On these three 'pillars' the play would seem to be built: the order and content of the other scenes would seem conditioned by these. Thus the architecture of the play seems intelligible only if thought of as proceeding, so to speak, from the central scenes outwards. The pose, and the cure, are given in the sources, so is the reason for the pose. The details that Molière had to add to this would not call for great imaginative power. The real invention would lie in transfusing the silly action into a suggestive picture, that means in penetrating the material with critical intelligence, in seeing what was involved in the facts, how they could be fitted into an order that would not be trivial, that would interest and provoke an audience with no interest in the actual matter.

Close study of the delicious opening scene reveals some realism, but more rhythm. Each quality seems 'just right'. There are homely touches to convince us (for the moment) that these are peasants; there is a technique of riposte in the dialogue that conveys a delight which a peasant's conversation could not give. This is obvious in the theatre and should be so to the critic. Each remark is a springboard (*tremplin*) for the reply. The Italians from whom Molière learnt to act would not even write the replies, but (like music-hall comedians of today) would work on an understanding: the one would launch a point, the other would cap it, and so on, each point needing only a single reply. This ballet trick is done here to perfection (I give the operative words of ten cases to show what I mean):

M. Non, je te dis . . .
S. Et je te dis, moi . . .
S. . . . qu'Aristote a bien raison . . .
M. Voyez l'habile homme avec son benêt d'Aristote . . .
S. Oui, habile homme . . . trouve-moi un faiseur de fagots qui sache raisonner . . .
M. Peste . . .
S. Peste . . .
M. Que maudit soit . . .
S. Que maudit soit . . .
S. . . . tu fus bien heureuse . . .
M. Qu'appelles-tu bien heureuse . . .
M. . . . Un homme qui me mange tout ce que j'ai.
S. . . . j'en bois une partie,
M. qui me vend tout dans le logis . . .
S. c'est vivre de ménage.
M. Qui m'a ôté jusqu'au lit . . .
S. Tu t'en lèveras plus matin.
M. Qui ne laisse aucun meuble . . .
S. On en déménage plus aisément.
M. J'ai quatre enfants sur les bras.
S. Mets-les à terre.

This passage alone justifies some conclusions: it is not haphazard: there is a principle of structure involved. Nor is it observed; such a conversation could not possibly take place. It is imagined. We are dealing with disciplined fantasy. And so through the play. The series have the look of realism; they have the balance of art. A progression such as this: ivrogne, sac-à-vin, infâme, traître, trompeur . . . is punctured, at every step, by this:

frotterai, battrai, rosserai, étrillerai. . . . Ah . . . .' The effect is produced by repetition in series; it would seem to require, and to assume, speed in the performance. As in the film, pictures are flashed before us, sometimes by single words. They are real enough while they last, and are not meant to last long. The effect is kaleidoscopic, of changing colours rather than of continuity, plot or development along a single line. In thus exploiting what he had himself been taught Molière was, all unawares, affecting the classical esthetic. The speed of the language allowed a larger range of matter to be included than was possible in tragedy or novel. Comedy has always claimed to talk of many things. With this new technique it could, and did, include the unpleasant without spoiling the effect of pleasure.

Study of the central scenes of *Le Médecin malgré lui* suggests an order and a design in the handling of the material that one cannot suppose it naturally had, or would have had in other hands. The effect is that of a critical intelligence that treats in some sort of order the various comic facets of the subject, reminding one of what Rudler called 'l'art des gradations' in *La Princesse de Clèves*. The basic *donnée* or datum, the ignoramus turned doctor, assumes ignorance, and calls for a pretence of knowledge. To keep this up, without actual knowledge, the quack has to simulate the manner, the professional comment, the refusal to be surprised or defeated by the evidence. All this Sganarelle does, to our pleasure. But he slips up, to our greater pleasure. And above all, and even more delightfully, he is conscious of his role, moves his mask to comment in a human way. Thus we may study the emergence of one of the immortal phrases of Molière, embedded as it were in its natural setting. As we hear it quoted we may well think it a chance quip that a quack should misplace the heart in the body. But part of the joke is that the first venture into anatomy risked by Sganarelle brings him at once to exposure, but not to decomposure. He carries off the grossest of blunders with the assurance: 'Nous avons changé tout cela, et nous faisons maintenant la médecine d'une méthode toute nouvelle'. Sganarelle is so sure of his professional authority that he can 'pardon' the interruption that exposes his ignorance: 'Il n'y a point de mal et vous n'êtes pas obligé d'être aussi habile que nous.' 'Habile' indeed, but in one sense for the enquirer, in quite another for Sganarelle, and for the audience.

So one could show how the elements of the comedy are distributed. The man who assumes knowledge of causes, of learned language and professional phrases is, when we see him off duty so to speak, sensual, witty, natural. The real and the unreal elements of the situation are so constantly interchanged that we are put in a world of fantasy, where all is, or may be, make-believe. In the situation treated as real, nothing is real (is not this a principle of all drama?). The girl is not dumb; Sganarelle is not a doctor; he does not know Latin; he does not know anything of what he is supposed to be master. Yet he *is* master, of the situation, by wit, by specious language, by flights into the unintelligible, by the barefaced assumption of non-existent authority. And it works. Why? Because it is applied to a realm where the layman cannot test the facts; he is reduced to believing the language, as a kind of magic. But who could put things in this way, arousing this reaction, unless he were possessed of ironic and critical intelligence and also of the gift of fantasy?

This kind of fantastic setting, so frequent in Molière,

we could almost assign on internal evidence to a stage in European culture that we might call pre-Enlightenment, when there is much questioning of the categories of knowledge, much testing of phenomena, when it is widely felt that the old categories will not do, that the traditional explanations are not to be trusted. *Le Médecin malgré lui* is not a parable of this state of mind, not even a satire of those who resisted it, but an imaginative entertainment by a man conscious of it, enjoyed by people who also would appreciate its 'angle'. It is in this sense alone that we might say that Molière is a thinker, that he prepares the way for Bayle and the new age, not by his ideas, but by his irony. What Bayle says learnedly, with masses of quotes and facts, Molière suggests ironically, without any facts. The poet was not out of touch with the intellectual temper of his time.

Study of the elements that make up the comedy suggests that professors who have praised the realism of Molière have been less near the mark than the actors who have questioned it. These rapid snapshots are not as lifelike as, when shown to us at speed, they seem to be; they have the life of art, they seem to be the comic counterpart of tragic symbols: they show one thing and suggest others. As satire they would be ponderous, which is just what they are not. Let us look at the doctors' discussion in *L'Amour Médecin*, at their love of procedure, rules, etiquette, academic discipline, even in matters of life and death: 'Un homme mort n'est qu'un homme mort, et ne fait point de conséquence; mais une formalité négligée porte un notable préjudice à tout le corps des médecins.' Did the doctors of Paris deserve this? Learned works have been written to show that they did, or did not. And we still do not know. Nor does it matter. The point made is a

scandal to the reasonable mind, the perfect ironic comment on the blindness of professionalism, on the absurdity
of servitude to regulation. But it is the irony, the perfection of line, that gives the pleasure, not the occasion
nor the fancied targets of the irony. It is the general point
that the reader takes. It was Taine who first pointed out
how perfectly Macaulay had taken this particular point:

They therefore gave the command to Lord Galway, an
experienced veteran, a man who was in war what Molière's
doctors were in medicine, who thought it much more
honourable to fail according to rule, than to succeed by innovation, and who would have been very much afraid of himself
if he had taken Monjuick by means so strange as those which
Peterborough employed. This great commander conducted
the campaign of 1707 in the most scientific manner. On the
plain of Almanga he encountered the army of the Bourbons.
He drew up his troops according to the methods prescribed
by the best writers, and in a few hours lost eighteen thousand
men, a hundred and twenty standards, all his baggage and all
his artillery.[2]

If all this be not too far from the mark, we should look
in each play for the dramatic centre, studying the structure
of those scenes that seem to command the rest, and then
observe how from such a dominant point the rest is
ordered. This is not arbitrarily to pick out a theme within
the play, nor to watch only its main figure. It has been
said of *Le Misanthrope* that it would seem a different play
if one were to consider the sub-title as well as the title.
Even more would it seem different if one were to study
the order and plan of scenes within the Acts. Those who
will may find in it the picture of an idealist in society, or
even a portrait of the author, but all such interpretations
are subjective and uncontrollable. They neglect large

[2] Macaulay, *Essays*, apud Taine, *Littérature anglaise*, v. 188.

blocks of comic material. They treat as incidental, and thus as not part of the main subject: the sonnet scene, the Marquis, and Arsinoé, to take only a few omissions. Unless the structure is bungled, all these have their place in the fiction. They are as much a part of the *ensemble* as is the main figure himself. Study of the play should surely include attention to the fact that this figure starts the play by expressing to a friend views that would make him seem ridiculous in any salon of the day. Is it accidental that he should be made to appear in a salon, and that before doing so, he should be shown in sharp conflict with two people? Is this order of scenes an accident? If so then it may be also an accident that the same interviews are repeated in slightly different order in the latter part of the play. But of course it is not accident; all is design, and our pleasure is increased if we take the entire suggestion of the play as it proceeds. What is it that opposes Alceste to the others? His views are different, but shared by them in some degree and certainly respected by them. It is clearly his tone, his manner, his temper, his rudeness when as so often he is put out. The man who could be so considerate and so naturally polite to Oronte (until he got annoyed) is impossible in a drawing room: 'Et moi, je soutiens, moi.' . . . Do idealism and sincerity need such rudeness? Do they require this mania for non-conformity, no less blind and arrogant than it is high-principled? They do not. This man is naive. He assumes that to speak one's mind is to speak the truth. But others speak their mind in this play. Acaste speaks his mind in a masterpiece of comic fatuity, Oronte speaks his mind, and would not do so if he knew how much he was saying. Arsinoé speaks her mind with malevolence, and with that spite which made Oscar Wilde's Gwendolen say that to criticise others was not merely a duty, but a pleasure. This mysterious and comic figure never comes anywhere near a true view of himself. Like Meredith's *Egoist*, written by an admirer of this play, he is wrapped in a cloud of self-righteousness. That someone else might be right about poetry, or judged right in the courts, or approved by Célimène, these things do not pierce his self-absorption. But these things are shown to us. We shall find that the encounters are significantly chosen and ordered and that the form of the play can give it the coherence that other plays get from plot or character.

This perhaps brings us to the chief result of detailed study of the language and structure of these plays, the discovery that all the poetic suggestions of the play occur within a form. That form seems to suggest the same question as the *École des Femmes* suggested: where all parties are ironically presented ('sie stellen sich dar und stellen sich bloß zugleich', said Vossler of Racinian characters) who then is the fool? All the others, says Alceste, and shows himself a fool for thinking so. Tartuffe's answer is much the same; his master is supposed to be the fool (and this was Molière's role) but in the final version of the play the artist has shown as with Arnolphe that to claim superior powers is to lose sight of one's own nature. So the man who could risk such an accurate description of himself as this:

> Tout le monde me prend pour un homme de bien
> Mais la vérité pure est que je ne vaux rien

only because he was confident that he would not be believed, that same man comes to express complete immorality in front of Elmire, and is thus seen by all to be, what he had unguardedly said he was. Again we have to look carefully at this. We shall not find it to be satire, in the first instance, or profound psychology (La Bruyère found it unrealistic) but part of a comic design, within a form.

In so difficult a matter and with regard to a play as powerful as *Tartuffe* one perhaps should say briefly the conclusion to which study of form leads. There is, I suggest, in *Tartuffe* a dramatic centre, a point round which everything seems to revolve. It is not an event, it is a point of view. I believe it may be found in the word *apparence* and its opposite. It is used at least five times in the play, at significant points: 'confondre l'apparence avec la vérité' is almost a motto. This is what the fool does; this is what the crook wants everyone to do. This is what his enemies are most concerned to get straight. The crook himself, in some ways Molière's finest creation, is presented from two angles: what he looks like, and what he is. The fool believes in what he looks like, and has to be convinced of what he is. All other characters either believe in him convinced by the 'apparence', or detest him suspecting the reality. There are thus four blocks of comic material presented as a pattern. We are shown the dissembler, in III, 2 and 6, and in IV, 1. We are shown the real man in III, 3 and in IV, 5 and 7. The dupes and the critics face each other in the first two Acts and the first part of the last. This shifting series of oppositions is at once so dramatic that events are hardly needed, and so symbolical that the impact of the unpleasant and the vicious is blunted and can be seen in larger perspective.

Even if it be granted that Molière creates a form in comedy, this will not seem important to the many who think that content is more important than form. What is the play about? How often is this thought to be the main question! The true answer is that only through the form can we know what the play is about. By considering what is often called the content, or subject matter, scholars have missed the comedy and magnified the satire. But it is possible to see what kind of situations this poet preferred to dramatise. He seems to have preferred situations where artfulness is defeated by artlessness. This may be to say no more than that he knew the taste of his public. I think we may add that he also knew his own power of portraying a fool, a butt, a dupe, a servant. Whatever the reason, it is a feature we should not miss. One of his most discerning critics has written:

Le principal thème du comique dramatique de Molière est le jeu entre la sottise et la ruse . . . la sottise alliée à la ruse . . . la ruse devenant sottise.[3]

As he imagined both these types, so Molière played them both. In so doing he was in an established tradition going back through the middle ages to ancient times. But to both types he gave new life. His fools are not just foolish; they are delightful. His pictures of folly suggest a fund (or 'fond') of nature, often of kindliness, certainly of humanity, which gives to the meanest intelligence a certain dignity. Chaplin in his stress on the dignity of the common man seems to come nearest to Molière in this respect. Even Harpagon, 'l'humain de tous les humains le moins humain' has to love something: Charles Dullin used to attach importance to the final glimpse of this character clutching his 'chère cassette'. This same gift is seen in the rich humanity of Jourdain, in his unsophisticated reactions, in his uninhibited vanity. It animates Chrysale no less, determined to fill his role as

[3] V. Vedel, op. cit., p. 476.

master of the house, soft-hearted to the dismissed servant, terrified of his able wife: 'Secondez-moi bien tous' as she comes in.

The knave is not so obvious a comic type. He has to be defeated, in the old comedy as in modern novels. Molière attains this objective by an invention which alters the character of comedy, that is by making the knave go too far, trust too much in his knavery, neglect his other qualities, and thus be the architect of his own downfall. In the ruin of their schemes these figures achieve some sort of humanity. This is true surely of Arnolphe, of Tartuffe, of Harpagon, and in some measure of Dom Juan and Alceste. It is suggested in the famous line from *Tartuffe*:

Ah, pour être dévot, je n'en suis pas moins homme.

The knave in whose mouth it is put would never admit to its full truth. Is it a pointer to common features of classical drama that this line should be copied from Corneille, whose Sertorius was anxious to show qualities other than military? Tartuffe's plan, like that of Arnolphe, is ruined by his sensuality. Alceste curses his love, which is his most human quality. This role of love is thus a major factor in the way in which Molière sets his comic scene. It seems to serve as antidote or counterpoise to qualities of will and brain, to qualities more ingenious and less natural. It would be worth study to follow this kind of distinction from the pages of Montaigne to the fantasies of Molière. One of the most interesting developments of the knave is seen in Molière's version of the Don Juan legend. He portrays him as far from distasteful, but entirely immoral, or amoral, as an aristocrat, of pleasant manners, who insists on his pleasure, who will admit no obligation, to women, to parents, to tradesmen, to God. It is strange that scholars have seen no form in a play that submits a character in turn to these symbols of the moral life. The central concept was the contemporary type known as 'l'esprit fort'. But his force, as La Bruyère later said of theirs, is illusory: he depends on the obligation of his valet to serve him, of his ladies to please him, of his father to believe him, of his tradesman to supply him: of his God who damns him he never speaks save to say that the words from Heaven are not clear. 'Quel homme', as the valet says, and we echo. The picture was too strong meat for the authorities but is now being recognised as having great dramatic power, and not nearly as obscure as Lemaître said it was.

If we had read no books about classical comedy we should not describe Molière as a man of reason nor as a profound psychologist. Both those things may be true, there is no space to argue them here, but there are more obvious features of his dramatic creation, an imaginative grasp of human nature and an astonishing sense of the dramatic.

It is a surprising fact that these plays so hurriedly put together, with such limitations of time and space for their performance, should have such permanence, such abiding suggestiveness, such frequent glimpses into the depths of existence and into the mystery of life. Molière's prime quality, it has been said, was 'son incapacité de rester à la surface'. The 'reversals' of which we have spoken are haunting as one recalls them: Tartuffe beginning with his pose of sanctity and ending in praise of secret sin and with a threat to Orgon to clear out of his own house. Trissotin, like Célimène with Arsinoé, and Alceste with Oronte, begins politely and ends with insults, and the insults seem more natural than the politeness. Argan reckons up the cost of his medicines cunningly but before long he is shivering at the thought of dying unattended, and asking if it is not dangerous to sham death. There is no theory proclaimed here, but a most sharp discernment into the layers of our human nature.

And the profundity of the comic artist is more than even these dramatic moments. 'J'ai pour moi la justice et je perds mon procès' seems a naive remark until we recognize in it the very human complaint that the ideal and the real rarely meet, that justice is proclaimed but rarely done. *George Dandin*, what a violent picture of the abyss between what should be and what is. Take what measures he will to establish his cause, which is just, the outcome mocks him and goads him to despair and into questioning the nature of things. In *Dom Juan* the simple man with no power of argument is often right where the clever arguer is wrong, just because most of us agree against the clever man that it is inhuman to believe . . . nothing. 'Encore faut-il croire quelque chose.' This is said by a valet yet is it not an ultimate reaction to scepticism? The attempt to live without sanctions, as Vardes and de Guiche and others were notorious for doing, is here condemned (as most people would condemn it) as impiety.

As works of art the comedies impress less perhaps by their profundity than by their rapidity. Speed seems the rule of this type of drama. The restlessness of Molière on and off stage aroused comment. Harpagon is like him in the way he rages at any obstacle. Even his language is too hurried to be grammatical: 'Rends-le-moi sans te fouiller.' But speed is a factor in comedy that has not been sufficiently studied. It has a close relation to the spirit of comedy. If, as has been said, comedy is an act of judgement, allowing an intellectual view of things juxtaposed, then two things are essential: that the pictures shown to us be vivid, and that they be quickly removed so that the mind may not dwell on their implications. The comic artist aims to show contour, shape, silhouette, 'le dessein', as Molière himself said, which explains why implications and developments matter less in comedy than in tragedy. Beginners often sympathise with Alceste because he has chosen the wrong girl. But pity is excluded from comedy, as is intimacy with characters or feelings. So that the starkest things may be suggested, as if in passing, con-nections are established between things of a different order, unhindered by the other conditions which in actual encounters always exist. Molière goes far in this direction. He suggests lubricity in *Tartuffe*, lunacy in *L'Avare*, and suicide in *George Dandin*. In *Amphitryon* even the question of identity of personality is raised, but lightly. This means that we do not consider these things as likely to happen, even within the illusion, and we are free to watch the idea as an intellectual proposition. *Dandin* is the best example of this feature. We recall that the play ends with the husband's disgust: 'Plus de remède . . . le meilleur parti qu'on puisse prendre, c'est de s'aller jeter dans l'eau.' We may say that he speaks so because he is a stupid man, but that makes no difference to the suggestion that there are times when such is 'le meilleur parti'. In our own day M. Camus has written that suicide is the only serious philosophical problem, since it implies a decision 'si la vie vaut ou ne vaut pas la peine d'être vécue'. Kafka has made similar points. Is not Molière, within the framework of a very different tradition, raising the same sort of issue? One returns in a final estimate to the power with which the material is intellectually imagined before being presented to us. 'L'événement n'obéit plus aux lois de la vie mais aux lois d'une réflexion' is the way in which one scholar expresses the work of a comic poet. This has not yet been studied. Things are presented in so natural a framework that they seem natural: such a figure as Jourdain does not seem, as he is, a brilliant creation of the critical imagination; he seems alive, and natural. People scoff at a climber and a sycophant, but at this climber nobody scoffs: his desire to copy the great seems so artless that we almost share it. Yet the author does not take his part against his wife. Both sides are presented fairly, and as they argue they touch on the old question:

Avez-vous envie qu'on se raille partout de vous?
—il n'y a que des sots et des sottes, ma femme, qui se railleront de moi.
—Il y a longtemps que vos façons de faire donnent à rire à tout le monde.
—Qui est donc ce monde-là s'il vous plaît?
—Tout ce monde-là est un monde qui a raison et qui est plus sage que vous.

Who are the fools? The Jourdains of the world? Or those who think them foolish? The question gets no answer; both sides have a case. Here in miniature is the comic dichotomy, which literature owes in its purest form to French classical comedy.

VI

THE
POWER OF PERSUASION

THE prose written by the French classical artists is an
ill-defined area of literature. The art of writing, as noted
above, concerned only poetry: the new novel was treated
as an offshoot of the epic. Of the traditional uses of prose,
as practised from ancient times in the west, the greater
French writers of the seventeenth century seem to have
taken little notice. Rhetoric, in the large sense of the
artistic ordering of speech, was as far from their concerns
as the narrower rhetoric of style and grammar. It could
almost be said that the French classical prose we admire
was written by accident. Neither Pascal nor Sévigné nor
Bossuet aimed to be 'literary'. They were hardly affected
by the rhetorical tradition, so alive in Spain through
writers like Gracián. Balzac, writing letters that in many
cases were not real letters, seems nearly alone in his care
for the art of writing. The famous *Art de Penser* of Port-
Royal, one of the most influential books of the age, is

indeed concerned with proper modes of expression but it is a competent rather than an inspired work.

To the great writers the content was more important than the form, though we should not think that Bossuet neglected the formal aspects of a sermon. But it is worth remark, that an age professing such regard for the Ancients should produce no lasting legal orations, nothing comparable in design to *Areopagitica* or *Urn-Burial*, no counterpart to Montaigne. These kinds of writing were not neglected. The speeches of Lemaître were admired, and published. Moral treatises still abound in the greater libraries. One scholar remarks that 'les moralistes pullulaient dans une société fort peu soucieuse de morale'. The ancient moralists and historians were read, and translated; Montaigne was probably well known to all the classical writers we are dealing with here. Is it an accident that no one of them attempted seriously to rival Juvenal (Boileau's occasional borrowings cannot be so described), or Cicero or Plutarch or Tacitus?

Pascal is the most remarkable of the French classical artists in prose. His style and phrasing have been studied, but the wider aspects of his writing hardly at all. He is a curious example of the distortion of a reputation by its supreme quality. Had he not been a religious genius, had the *Pensées* not been translated into many languages as devotional literature, they might have been studied for their imaginative and literary power. As it is, the content is labelled specialist, and the literary historian is left with 'the style'. Yet if classicism is more than elegant expression, if (whatever its full definition) it includes cogency and novelty of conception, then Pascal may well be (with Molière and Racine) its chief exponent.

Our judgement must rest on what he left unrevised,

since he published nothing except a series of pamphlets and some technical treatises. Yet he was clearly a master of polemic, as of epigram, and so original in his method of argument that his influence on writers of the late nineteenth century has required a special study.

When Antoine Arnauld suggested to the young scientist that he should take a hand in stating the Jansenist case in 1656 it may be that he had been impressed by the sketch of a preface to a treatise on the vacuum planned some nine years earlier. This was never in fact published until Bossut included it in his edition of 1779. Yet in its way it is as important a work for the literary historian as the *Provinciales*. It is a discussion of the proper place of authority in science, and can be read today, without knowledge of the polemics that accounted for its writing, as a masterly statement of the question, firmly based on seventeenth-century assumptions but retaining some of its original force, and at once more clear and more relevant than the better known treatise with which d'Alembert prefaced the *Encyclopédie*. This *Fragment d'une Préface à un Traité du Vide*[4] is a personal and violent piece of writing. Its author had clearly been stung by refusal to accept his experiments, on the ground that the authority of ancient principle (in that case, that nature abhors a vacuum) was to be respected in science as in other fields of knowledge. Pascal writes as a scientist whose experiments have convinced him that *in this case* ancient principle was wrong. He writes as a man of religion who had been horrified by a recent attempt to abandon similar principles in theology. He confronts a practical issue and seeks a way out of an apparent impasse. The principle of authority seemed essential: without it the Christian religion might be

[4] Brunschvicg, ed. minor, pp. 74–83.

argued away. Yet this same principle was blocking a clear way forward in science. Pascal's answer is a perfect piece of classical polemic. He applies to his problem an argument that he could (and probably did) find in the *Augustinus*, that no single principle should be applied to all the known sciences. Certain sciences were to be acquired by memory, others by reasoning, yet others, added Pascal, by experiment. In some sciences principles were clearly laid down from the start, as in theology by revelation. It is amusing to find Pascal including among the sciences of memory jurisprudence, history and geography. He seems to have had no suspicion that in these fields ancient statements either could or should be questioned. Here he was a man of his age, and his task was harder than that of d'Alembert a century later. A second category of sciences included those, like mathematics, where certain principles were clear, leaving the implications to be deduced from them. In natural sciences, since 'the secrets of nature are hidden', both reason and experiment were needed.

Pascal proves his point easily but the real interest of his writing lies elsewhere. It lies in the fact that the force of his argument took him further than he wished to go. On the surface his position is cartesian. Descartes admitted the value of experiment, but in his discussions with Harvey he showed that he thought experiment should confirm principles reached by argument. Pascal says outright that 'les expériences sont les seuls principes de la physique'. That is, in physics, he is content to do without general principles, and to be led, step by step, according to particular cases. For Descartes this was not science at all; it was piecemeal investigation. But Pascal (and surely by reason of the heat of his argument) is led to enunciate the inductive method. One scholar indeed has claimed that 'Pascal se sert de la méthode inductive dans toute sa perfection'. If this be going too far, we can at least see how the desire to defend his discovery had made him aware of a method that goes beyond the cartesian method of reasoning from a fixed point, a method that starts from the particular fact and allows experiments to suggest a general hypothesis, which in turn is confirmed or altered by yet more experiments. Is not this the method of most modern scientists? Pascal may be said to have stumbled upon it, since in his *Fragment* he was not concerned to find a new method but to justify a precise activity. In doing that he found that he had to assert the necessity of authority in theology, which was not new, and the necessity of experiment in physics, which was new. Nor did the matter end for him there. As later he reflected on ways of explaining religion he brought into play arguments of a personal and existential kind, where he felt that traditional arguments from authority and revelation were likely to have no effect. Thus the *Fragment* suggests some of the most original insights of the *Pensées*.[5]

One other scientific treatise, also unpublished, contains ingredients of the later *Apology*. It has been preserved in two parts, and is known as 'De L'Esprit Géométrique'. It is a plea for mathematical method in matters other than mathematical. Perfectly conducted arguments being impossible, since all things cannot be defined, let us define only those things not immediately perceptible as true. Pascal's development of this point is possibly more valuable for his type of apologetic than as a philosophical

[5] For a fuller discussion of this, to my mind neglected, matter see my article 'Pascal and the Scientific Spirit', *Cambridge Journal*, 1954.

position. He regards all precision as medial and limited. As in mathematics we have to assume unprovable starting-points, that we call axioms, and as we have to deal with measures of time and quantity that run in both directions into infinity (since we can always imagine one more or one less than a given number) then both the origin and end of things are beyond our grasp. Is it any wonder that an *Apology* for religion by a man trained in this kind of argument has proved powerful with the unorthodox? These pages show Pascal already prepared to consider other means of persuasion than rational argument. Thus

> En parlant des choses humaines on dit qu'il faut les connaître avant que de les aimer . . . les saints au contraire disent en parlant des choses divines qu'il faut les aimer pour les connaître.

These short treatises suggest a type of thinking that we can trace at work in the apparently very different *Lettres Provinciales*. The polemic of the famous letters owes its main force to the skill with which every issue is simplified, dramatised, so presented that clarity seems convincing and complexity appears ridiculous. Experts who are asked for the facts give themselves away by their muddled explanations and by their unintentional confusions. Because of their general position they are made to state and to defend particular propositions at the extremes of casuistry and which are point by point exposed by the full rigour of scripture. Thus the Jesuit father:

> Je veux maintenant vous faire voir cette grande méthode dans tout son lustre sur le sujet de l'homicide, qu'elle justifie en mille rencontres, afin que vous jugiez par un tel effet tout ce qu'elle est capable de produire . . . .

For the equivalent of such irony one must go to Swift and to Molière. It is perhaps significant that Molière adapts this very passage of the 7th *Provinciale*. In Pascal's hands innocence is deceptive and naiveté a mask:

Aussitôt qu'il m'aperçoit, il vint à moi et me dit, en regardant dans un livre qu'il tenait à la main: Qui vous ouvrirait le paradis, ne vous obligerait-il pas parfaitement? . . .

But the whole method is brilliantly illustrated in the very first Letter, in the passage on the word *suffisant*, which they agree not to define, so divergent are the attempts to give it any meaning. In literary terms this deliberately dramatic alteration of the actual theological issue means that a point is created and pressed home, a point that goes beyond the discussions Pascal had in mind and which he was more concerned to ridicule than to reproduce. Almost the same point is made by T. S. Eliot, in speaking of democracy: 'When a term has become so universally sanctified as democracy now is, I begin to wonder whether it means anything, in meaning so many things.'

This is a feature we have met before. The vigour of the argument pushes the scene out of context. We retain its essence and forget its occasion, as Macaulay did with the scene from *L'Amour Médecin*. These writers have discovered a way of holding, in ironic sterilization as it were, a human pose. So here, the attitude of constant resistance to casuistry, of constant and relentless enquiry into plain meaning, applied to things which are and must be the reverse of plain, itself induces an attitude, a set of criteria. The necessity of polemic forces Pascal into the mould so to speak of the layman, who demands an explanation. His attack on the abuse seems often an attack on authority itself, however much he may protest the contrary. 'Les Provinciales,' said Sainte-Beuve, 'ont tué les Jésuites, et bien d'autres choses encore.' Pascal has written what he did not probably intend to write, a non-conformist book; he has assumed a secular attitude, from which later and bolder spirits will take their tone. 'Pascal a frayé la voie à Voltaire', said Lanson, meaning no doubt that where one has struck such blows, others are encouraged to do so, and to go further. Is this the famous objectivity of classicism? It looks more like the heat of controversy, dangerous, unfair, powerful. In Taine's day the fact was recognised by the refusal to enter the book in the catalogue of the Ecole Normale library, although the students made full use of the actual library copy.

It would be possible to show how, in the fragments known as the Pensées, these qualities of irony and antithesis achieve impressive effects. The dramatic sense of opposing forces, so often found within the classical alexandrine verse, is here expressed in mordant pictures of the human condition. The force of the prose lies in comparison, contrast, antithesis. This was in the Provinciales forced to serve a case. It seems much less so in the Pensées. The prose is dramatic because two things seem present in the author's mind: the sense of human claims, and the sense of human limits. Neither is often expressed without the other. Together they make for perfect expression of an age which was itself their meeting point, an age of faith and tradition, but an age of achievement and vision no less. A ship adrift is not in itself a classical, nor a baroque, image; it seems to have the effect of both, when applied to the human condition. Images, like the arguments, change and oppose each other: a ship adrift, with no anchorage, tall towers menaced by earthquake:

Nous voguons sur un milieu vaste, toujours incertains et flottants, poussés d'un bout vers l'autre. Quelque terme où nous pensions nous attacher et nous affermir, il branle et nous quitte; et si nous le suivons il échappe à nos prises, nous glisse et fuit d'une fuite éternelle. Rien ne s'arrête pour nous. C'est l'état qui nous est naturel, et toutefois le plus contraire à notre inclination; nous brûlons de désir de trouver une assiette ferme, et une dernière base constante pour y édifier une tour qui s'élève à l'infini, mais tout notre fondement craque, et la terre s'ouvre jusqu'aux abîmes.

I think that Mr. Friedrich is right, and the stylistic analysts are wrong who say that these are in a strict sense pictures: 'Bilder sind das nicht . . . es sind intensiv gewordene Abstracta.' Such existential writing must perforce be dramatic. The facts and the reflection are in constant conflict. The mind misleads: as a guide it has to be corrected by nature:

Que fera donc l'homme? Doutera-t-il s'il doute? Doutera-t-il s'il est? On n'en peut venir là, et je mets en fait qu'il n'y a jamais eu de pyrrhonien effectif parfait. La nature soutient la raison impuissante, et l'empêche d'extravaguer jusqu'à ce point. . . . Qui démêlera cet embrouillement? La nature confond les pyrrhoniens, et la raison confond les dogmatiques . . . Connaissez donc, superbe, quel paradoxe vous êtes à vous-même. . . .

Molière seems to think of reason and nature in much this way, yet in both cases the paradox is more than theatrical; it is purposive. Both writers convey a sense that the whole man is more than mind. The suggestion of the unified sane personality which is the basis of the laughter in Molière, is similar to the awareness in Pascal of scientific order and category, as in the beautiful passage on the three orders[6], or the way that the God of the Bible satisfies in us not only 'la part des philosophes et des savants' but the doubter and the penitent.[7]

It is I think a shallow view that regards the *Apology* attempted in the *Pensées* as out-of-date because the proofs fail to convince. Pascal suggests that all proofs at some stage fail to convince. He aims less at conviction than at persuasion: 'l'instrument par lequel la persuasion se fait n'est pas la seule démonstration. Combien y a-t-il peu de choses démontrées.' His *Apology* certainly is out-of-date in those parts where the science of biblical criticism has altered the state of the matter. But much is left unaffected. No religious apologist before him, I believe, put such stress on inclination, will, habit, on seeking as well as finding, in instinct as well as ignorance. These dual emphases give to his writing a resonance that seems quite unusual. He writes as an intellectual, who has been made aware of the limitations of the intellectual. As in fact he had. 'C'est un mathématicien qui ne sait que cela', said an acquaintance of him. As if attempting to correct this he wrote a page (which provoked Samuel Pepys to a translation) exploring the difference between types of mind, the logical and the intuitive, the *esprits géométriques* who think consequently, and the *esprits de finesse* who think in flashes of insight. The intuitive came to be a major concept for him: 'C'est le cœur qui sent Dieu . . . le cœur a ses raisons que la raison ne connaît pas.' This last phrase is so widely used that it has come adrift from its author: I have heard it ascribed to Mr. Churchill.

Pascal is not often spoken of as a classical writer. Bossuet, on the contrary, is for many the finest writer of

---

[6] Br. 793
[7] 553, 556

French classical prose. To pass from the one to the other is at first a deceptive experience, as if one were leaving the realm of the *esprit de finesse* for the *esprit de géométrie*. Pascal's mastery of ideas is such as to make passages in Bossuet appear as grandly articulated commonplaces. This is unfair. Bossuet was one of the most intelligent and consequent thinkers of his time; his intellectual grasp is firmer than would at first appear. His misfortune is that he was representative of traditional thinking, and that he championed ideas which were then perfectly valid, but which have come to look absurdly limited. The movement of thought has been such as to put him almost invariably on the wrong side. He stood for tradition against innovation, at a point in history where innovation was to have it all its own way for two hundred years. He read history as a series of proofs of divine providence. He thought the Revocation a good thing, though he did what he could to diminish its brutality. He fought for the truth, but for him that was to fight against scientific enquiry, against deviation from tradition. In his eyes to 'vary' was to err; his attitude in all his controversies might be not unfairly summed up as the complete contrary of Renan's principle: 'le moyen de ne pas varier est de ne pas penser'. He took this so far as to commit himself to the view (in a directive of 1700) that 'l'hérétique est celui qui a une opinion'. Yet despite all this he was closer to Pascal's outlook than we realise. Both abhorred protestantism nearly as much as incredulity; both were hostile to scientific study of scripture; both believed Genesis to state the truth about the origin of man on earth. If asked both would have said that to be a Seeker in religion was not enough, though Pascal has much about seeking and Bossuet finds the very notion an absurdity:

ceux qu'on nomme chercheurs à cause que dix sept cents ans après Jesus Christ ils cherchent encore la religion et n'en ont point d'arrêtée.

Not only did these two men share a general view of the world; they each had qualities that were capable of animating prose style. If Pascal has the sharper dialectic, Bossuet has the temperament of the born controversialist, never losing sight of the main issue, never confusing the issue with the opponent, always courteous, always restrained, human and balanced where Pascal is violent and extreme. The strength of his character seems to have something to do with the texture of his reasoning. His most famous pulpit performances have been unfairly called 'chefs-d'œuvre d'un genre faux', unfairly because one of their characteristics is the absence of flattery, their concern to bring home to lords and kings the basic truths of mortality. He is the very opposite of a sycophant. His prose is vigorous because he has a clear view and a simple faith. He describes events with great effect because he thinks that events show an eternal pattern. His account of Cromwell is effective because for him Cromwell is a man sent from God, albeit as a scourge. (His view of events is not in fact very different from Cromwell's own view.)

There are reasons why pulpit eloquence may be thought to have much in common with what is called the classical manner. The Christian preacher looks at the human situation, puts the case of all men, is moved by what affects all men: misfortune, error, mortality. His canvas is that of life in the large; in his picture the particular features seem submerged in the general and the universal. But this generalisation may be deceptive. Consider a famous passage:

Je veux dans un seul malheur déplorer toutes les calamités du genre humain, et dans une seule mort faire voir la mort et

le néant de toutes les grandeurs humaines. . . . Après ce que
nous venons de voir, la santé n'est qu'un nom, la vie n'est
qu'un songe, la gloire n'est qu'une apparence, les grâces et les
plaisirs ne sont qu'un dangereux amusement: tout est vain en
nous, excepté le sincère aveu que nous faisons devant Dieu
de nos vanités, et le jugement arrêté qui nous fait mépriser tout
ce que nous sommes.

This is not a typical passage. It arises from the reflection
that nine months earlier the preacher had celebrated the
death of the mother in the presence of the daughter.
The speed with which death had struck the chief hearer of
the first sermon had made him resolve to look no further
for a text and a theme than the opening words of Ecclesi-
astes. He is less concerned to generalise death than to
seize its symbolic power. There is something here quite
different from the *lieux communs* of contemporary tragedy.
As we seek for a principle behind these imposing sentences
we note that without the Pascalian dialectic they make
constant use of the principle that seems to govern much
seventeenth-century prose, the vivid opposition of ideas.
This after all is natural to any preacher. Concerned to
convey the sense of an unseen reality he will be for ever
contrasting what is temporal and what is eternal, the
apparent and the real, this world and the next. Much of
Bossuet's prose seems to depend on this contrast. He
delights to contrast the weakness of man and the power
of God, the chances and changes of life with the change-
lessness of God, brevity and mortality against eternity.
He has made, as no other Frenchman has ever done, his
language to be a vehicle of such themes. Close study
suggests not so much elaboration of the commonplace as
concentration on a relationship, of imagination seeking
the symbol. Consider the famous passage from the early

sermon on the conversion of Saint Bernard; the vivid soliloquy put in the mouth of the young saint is much more than a homily on the passage of time:

Hélas, on ne parle que de passer le temps. Le temps passe en effet, et nous passons avec lui; et ce qui passe à mon égard par le moyen du temps qui s'écoule, entre dans l'éternité qui ne passe pas; et tout se ramasse dans le trésor de la science divine qui ne passe pas. O Dieu éternel, quel sera notre étonnement, lorsque le Juge sévère qui préside l'autre siècle, où celui-ci nous conduit malgré nous, nous représentant en un instant toute notre vie, nous dira d'une voix terrible: Insensés que vous êtes, qui avez tant estimé les plaisirs qui passent, et qui n'avez pas considéré la suite, qui ne passe pas.

If we count the grouping of syllables we may see that the preacher used breath groups of similar length to those of the alexandrine. If we watch the repetitions, they are not so much rhythmical as they are dramatic. The negative use of 'passer' in another context would appear cacophony. But the opposition underlying the sound is clear, constant, and urgently enforced by the repetition. It is an opposition of two attitudes, the judgement of man, and the judgement of God. The force of the final suggestion of the last Judgement is only the culminating instance of these imagined oppositions.

Exactly forty years later the old Bishop of Meaux wrote for Louise de Luynes, prioress of Torcy, a meditation on life hid in God, which at one point seems effortlessly to return to the basic contrast, this time as a picture of illusion and reality in the human person, what men think you are, as opposed to what you are in the sight of God.

Et votre vie est cachée . . . qu'on est heureux, qu'on est tranquille. Affranchi des jugements humains, on ne compte plus pour véritable que ce que Dieu voit en nous, ce qu'il en sait, ce qu'il en juge. Dieu ne juge pas comme l'homme; l'homme ne voit que le visage, que l'extérieur. Dieu pénètre le fond des cœurs, Dieu ne change pas comme l'homme; son jugement n'a point d'inconstance, c'est le seul sur lequel il faut s'appuyer: qu'on est heureux alors, qu'on est tranquille. On n'est pas ébloui des apparences; on a secoué le joug des opinions; on est uni à la vérité, et on ne dépend que d'elle.

On me loue, on me blâme, on me tient pour indifférent, on me méprise, on ne me connaît pas ou l'on m'oublie; tout cela ne me touche pas, je n'en suis pas moins ce que je suis; l'homme se veut mêler d'être créateur; il me veut donner un être dans son opinion ou dans celle des autres; mais cet être qu'il me veut donner est un néant. Car qu'est-ce qu'un être qu'on me veut donner, et qui néanmoins n'est pas en moi, sinon une illusion, une ombre, une apparence, c'est à dire dans le fond un néant? Qu'est ce que mon ombre qui me suit toujours, tantôt derrière, tantôt à côté? Est-ce mon être, ou quelque chose de mon être? Rien de tout cela . . . .[8]

We may note that the same theme seems here to take on the ease and maturity of experience, of a long life looked at almost from outside itself. The tone changes easily from the impersonal 'on', anybody, to the first person. This 'I' or 'me' may also apply to anybody but it leaves the reader free to introduce his own experience. Such writing is neither impersonal, nor limited to individual experience. It is a synthesis such as the seventeenth century made possible, and which the conventions of that age—the formal expression, the short sentences, the refusal to go beyond the given subject, to shock or to distract—made it possible to transmute from actual experience into ordinary and yet powerful words.

[8] Bossuet, *Extraits des Oeuvres Diverses*, ed. Lanson, 1899, pp. 465 ff. My first knowledge of this passage I owe to my colleague, Mr. A. Gill, of Magdalen College.

VII

THE SOUL OF WIT

In the full flight of one of her breathless descriptions Mme de Sévigné exclaims: 'Le moyen de tout dire?' It is almost the artist's question, and we have seen how the dramatists and others replied to it. But French classical literature was to provide quite an unexpected reply by cultivating the epigram. In a day that often confused quantity and quality, when 'imposing' works had to be long, there were not many who thought, with Alceste, that 'le temps ne fait rien à l'affaire', or with Pascal that the business of an author was to shorten his first draft. So it was daring to maintain that more could be said in few words than in many. The social game of formulating an opinion—such it seems to have been in its first stages—ended in the creation of jewels of speech in which ruthless pruning revealed an unqualified single point.

This novelty, for such it was, cultivated by a small circle of the French upper class, was also a recovery of a ancient tool of rhetoric. The Latin tradition in Europe, as Curtius has shown, lived on in the many medieval experiments to abbreviate, and to refine expression. What Curtius calls 'Kürze als Stilideal' was no invention of the seventeenth century, and in the middle ages it was probably more varied and subtle than his cases suggest. In popular speech it produced proverbs and 'dictons' which conceal the truth as much as they condense it. La Rochefoucauld could hear on his estates at Verteuil wise words about the crops or the market that rival in pungency any of his making. 'Entre faire et dire a moult', or 'Qui sage est doubte', for example, could be written in the margin of many of his own maximes. (For convenience I distinguish between maxim in the English sense, *maxime* as referring to La Rochefoucauld's creation and *Maximes* to the title of his book.) The medieval schools knew all about the *sententia* and the term was current in the seventeenth century for sayings of general import, much used in the new drama: the printed versions of plays often put such lines within quotation marks.

The attractions of brevity are many. As a variant to narration, and to the *amplificatio* demanded of the historian, the single pungent phrase is effective. To the usual qualities of prose, explanation, qualification, extension, it prefers absence of extenuation, sharpness of statement, shock, surprise, paradox. Truth becomes more pregnant when thus compressed, more cryptic when not explained. Nor is it always the truth. Rather *a* truth, an angle of vision, striking because we are unaccustomed to 'see it that way'. The epigram is allied to the proverb and to the riddle. It is the only modern genre that has preserved the delphic quality of 'dark' speech. Such an epigram as this 'La fortune et l'humeur gouvernent le monde' is shocking in its apparent injustice. This is not the truth, we feel. Yet, like the bent bow, it releases, with the pent-up force of the unexplained, *a* truth, *an* aspect which, without a shock, we would not entertain. That two qualities of which we do not think highly and which we tend to omit from our calculation should 'manage' the world, the shock of this reveals more effectively than any argument the unsuspected part that chance and mood do play in human affairs. The point is made by four operative words. The bounds of bare statement are reached here and they invite any reaction, as many examples as readers may offer. This is, in a way, a new way, poetic statement. Words are pointers; they do not stand for single things. The suggestive power of poetry is found here, perhaps more than in the verses of the time. In the hands of a master, this compression can do what ordinary statements cannot do: it can impel the mind beyond what is actually said. Is not this a seventeenth-century approach to Mallarmé's principle: 'to name is to destroy, to suggest is to create'?[9]

The suggestive power of single statement is usually associated with the name of La Rochefoucauld. But he worked along with others. And similar tendencies may be marked in novel and drama and in the polemic of Pascal. For such a writer as Guez de Balzac it was cultivated as an ornament. It seems to have been a feature of elegant conversation. Collections were made of sayings and anecdotes: they seemed to need no other description than their association with an individual, *Segraisiana* or *Menagiana*. These sayings and doings became matter of art in the hands of a younger contemporary of Pascal and Molière: La Bruyère gave new life to the epigram by setting it alongside the portrait or picture-epigram, and

[9] The actual formulation seems to belong to Symons rather than to Mallarmé. Cf. A. Symons, *The Symbolist Movement in Literature*, 1899, p. 132.

by composing paragraphs of unconnected single statements.

It may well have been Corneille who taught his
generation to savour pungent statement. He gave to the
single line a resonance and a distinction that set it apart
from the rest, and this was no doubt even more effective
in the recitation. Such a phrase as 'L'honneur est un
devoir; il est tant de maîtresses' suggests an attitude, and
more: it suggests *the* attitude in which the audience, like
Rodrigue (its immediate audience) require to be interested. The martyr is a dramatic figure, but how much
more so when a single statement can convey his own
insight into his paradoxical position of a living being
actually seeking death:

> Je consens, ou plutôt j'aspire, à ma ruine.

Molière refines on this dramatic pungency, by working a
character up to that pitch of exasperation where it will
unwittingly unload its own formula: 'Je ne suis pas bon,
je suis méchant quand je veux', or 'Nul n'aura de l'esprit
hors nous et nos amis'. This latter gem is not satire of
anyone: it is satire of all academism. 'Epouser une sotte
est pour n'être point sot' really conveys three things at
once: Arnolphe's desire to escape cuckoldry, his notion
that to marry a fool is not foolish, and the impression (on
us) that this ponderous 'wisdom' is the height of folly.
'Je ne suis pas bon, je suis méchant quand je veux' is not
what Argan, or anybody else would willingly reveal; it is
something that describes him (and us) far better than any
of the things that he means to say.

As a master of comedy, Molière had opportunities of
ambiguity and layers of meaning that writers in other
fields could not use. The proposition that brevity is the

soul of wit could be proved from his works alone. But the capacity for pregnant expression is not the same thing as actual cultivation of the epigram. The first is found to some extent in all the finer writing of the age. The second is a matter of deliberate cultivation and is carried to perfection by two or three. Pascal is master of both and suggests a relation between the one and the other.

The *Provinciales* contain many instances of an argument and an attitude being subsumed in a single cutting phrase: 'En vérité le monde devient méfiant et ne croit les choses que lorsqu'il les voit.' Or 'c'est ici une hérésie d'une nouvelle espèce: ce ne sont pas les sentiments de M. Arnauld qui sont hérétiques, c'est sa personne'. What is almost the last phrase of the 18th *Letter* reads as if it were entirely clear, yet it assumes the polemic of the previous letters: 'Laissez l'Eglise en paix et je vous y laisserai de bon cœur.' An even finer example is not from the *Letters* but from an unpublished fragment: describing the bees building their hive he puts in a line what his century thought animal instinct to be: 'La nature les instruit à mesure que la nécessité les presse'.[1]

I think this may fairly be called epigrammatic writing. It gives us the 'multum in parvo' quality without being itself epigram. We can see this if we put beside any just quoted this: 'Le cœur a ses raisons que la raison ne connaît pas.' This is a full statement, that suggests much evidence not given. The double use of so difficult a word as 'raison' in the space of a line might be thought confusing. But the possessive makes it a suggestive pointer to the existence of something not yet defined, things that do the work of reason yet are not reason. It is full, it is attractive, it is cryptic, it could serve as a guide to further

[1] ed. Brunschvicg minor, p. 79.

discussion. This notion of 'guide' is as it happens close
to the usual sense of the word *maxime*. La Bruyère says
he will not write in *maximes*, which are 'comme des lois
dans la morale', guiding lines in discussions of conduct.
The salons made much of these discussions. Mme de
Sablé even kept a secretary to record the neatest formu-
lations of what was thought to be worth preserving. The
novels show how fascinating was the search for the right
attitude to any event or person. In *La Prétieuse* by l'Abbé
de Pure, published in 1656 and probably known to La
Rochefoucauld, one such session begins thus:

Il n'y a point de plus injustes jugements que ceux que l'on
rend sur les faits d'amour . . . tout le monde juge mal de
l'amour.

This is probably the sort of setting that we should imagine
for such a maxime as La Rochefoucauld's number 70:

Il n'y a point de déguisement qui puisse longtemps cacher
l'amour où il est, ni le feindre où il n'est pas.

We should not think that the discussions were limited
to love or to manners. The famous 'Discours sur les
Passions de l'Amour', for some time attributed to Pascal,
would seem to be a collection of notes of such salon
conversations; it contains views on life and mind, and
even a sort of rationale of the maxime as a form of
expression:

L'on écrit souvent des choses que l'on ne prouve qu'en
obligeant tout le monde à faire réflexion sur soi-même et à
trouver la vérité dont on parle.

The expression of these things that would force people
to think afresh would seem to have had no rules. But to
judge from the cases still found it had recognized

objectives. The minimum of words was one of these; the use of key words was another. The effect of surprise was a third. A fourth was what La Bruyère called the quality of 'oracle': part of the attraction lay in the obscurity, the mystery of a delphic pronouncement. In aiming at this quality these French ladies and gentlemen were unwittingly returning to a very old tradition. Mr. Huizinga has written:

> The close connections between poetry and the riddle are never entirely lost. In the Icelandic skalds too much clarity is considered a technical fault. The Greeks also required the poet's word to be dark. Among the troubadours, in whose art the play function is more in evidence than any other, special merit was attributed to trobar clus, the making of recondite poetry. Modern schools of lyric, which move and have their beings in realms not generally accessible, are fond of wrapping the sense in an enigmatic word.

The enigmatic word, is there a place for this in a literature that has been praised for its sense of clarity? Such a word perhaps for Pascal was the quite ordinary term 'comprendre'. He puts its two normal senses together and we have:

> Par l'espace l'univers me comprend et m'engloutit
>   comme un point;
> Par la pensée je le comprends.

This is not clear in the sense of being immediately intelligible; perhaps it is not intelligible at all. But even if not, it is epigrammatic and mysterious. The verb in the first case has a clear meaning, but what about the second? Does not the attraction of the epigram spring precisely from this hesitation between two suggestions? By my thought I give meaning to the world, I understand it; do

I also embrace and encompass it? Had Pascal known the answer he would not have made the pun, and written what is an ambiguity, but one in which the sense is not so much faulty as overwhelming. Should we not feel much the same about La Rochefoucauld's No. 26:

> Le soleil ni la mort ne se peuvent regarder fixement.

This seems at first sight a most far-fetched comparison. We have heard death compared to almost everything but the sun. What have death and the sun in common? Nothing save the quality of dazzling the eye that would look at them without flinching. Death as dazzling, confusing, impenetrable, beyond our scrutiny, is this a profound insight? I would not think so, yet this single and bare comparison ruins at a stroke all that has been or that can be said about death. Since no living man has seen death, we may imagine things about it, none of us can know what we are actually talking about. This would seem to be a marvel of speech, that can combine in ten words an incentive to endless meditation. And this, surely is the great Anglo-Saxon tradition of epigram, the tradition of Sir Thomas Browne and Emerson and Nietzsche, the tradition that made Stevenson say 'the obscurest epoch is today'. It was no less than contact with this tradition that was discovered in the salons of Paris in 1658.

We have not yet fully defined the maxime as epigram. 'Toutes les bonnes maximes sont dans le monde; on ne manque qu'à les appliquer.' When Pascal wrote this he was not thinking of epigrams, but of principles of conduct. These contain two elements: a sum of experience, and a piece of advice. The epigram as a work of art always contains the first element, but it rarely contains the second.

Most books of morals contain more of the second than the first. Arnolphe inflicted his 'Maximes de Mariage' on Agnés, ostensibly as the truths of experience, but really to tell her what to do, and even more what she should not do. Much of the potted wisdom of that age as of others was of this kind. Even the much-read Gracián, in the course of making epigrams, gives much advice, thus:

> Eviter les engagements. C'est une des principales maximes de la prudence . . . Un engagement en tire après soi un autre plus grand, et d'ordinaire le précipice est à côté . . . Mais celui qui a la Raison pour guide va toujours bride en main.

This is an example of the maxim as advice. But Gracián has also the maxim as epigram:

> La Science dépourvue du bon sens est une double folie.

We touch here perhaps one of the most durable misconceptions of French classical literature. The French have a great tradition of *moralistes*, a word which if translated literally into English alters in sense. The true translation would be something like analysts or psychologists, since they describe much more than they prescribe. Perhaps their work would have been more generally recognised as art if this difference had been made clear. La Rochefoucauld rarely if ever gives advice; he is always intent on describing how things are, how the world goes, what the real elements in a situation are. Indeed he knew that between advice about living and the art of living there is a great gulf fixed. So he wrote (No. 93):

> Les vieillards aiment à donner de bons préceptes, pour se consoler de n'être plus en état de donner de mauvais exemples.

The question of how such epigrams were actually manufactured has been argued back and forth ever since

Victor Cousin suggested over a century ago that the credit was due to the Marquise de Sable and her salon and that La Rochefoucauld merely followed a fashion. The known facts hardly warrant this notion. They suggest rather that with one or two others the Duke took the society game seriously and cultivated the art of expression. He refers frequently in letters to the work that this entailed, calling his epigrams usually 'sentences'. In a rather outspoken reflection of which he never sanctioned the publication he wrote: 'Il est aussi ridicule de vouloir faire des sentences sans avoir la graine en soi, que de vouloir qu'un parterre produise des tulipes quand on n'y a pas planté les oignons.'

The evidence also suggests that these *sentences* were not only the fruit of a special talent, but of discussion and argument. 'Vous savez bien que ce ne sont sentences qu'après que vous les avez approuvées,' he wrote once to the Marquise, even though, as Mr. Grubbs pointed out, he rarely took her advice. Nor did they spring to his mind in a happy thought. The earliest form shows them embedded in longer reflections. Indeed La Rochefoucauld's first writing of this kind is not a *maxime* at all but a long and eloquent account of self-interest, which he had come to regard as the prime motive of all behaviour. It is his finest piece of writing and shows not only a superb gift of expression but a concentration on phenomena of conduct that has never been credited to him. Some of the manuscript versions enable us to see the process of concentration and of 'filing down' actually going on:

Les crimes deviennent innocents, même glorieux, par leur nombre et par leurs qualités; de là vient que les voleries publiques sont des habiletés et que prendre des provinces injustement s'appelle faire des conquêtes. Le crime a ses héros ainsi que la vertu.

The last sentence is a *maxime*, explained by a reflection on current events. The explanation is withdrawn, leaving the *maxime* almost anonymous so to speak, without attachment to a single event. Even this formulation was considered too outspoken, so all that passed into later editions was No. 185: 'Il y a des héros en mal comme en bien.' This shows how far the final epigram can be from its starting point.

The cynical tone and the emphasis on self-interest have led scholars to speak as if La Rochefoucauld had wished to destroy belief in virtue. This has been uncritically accepted and has concealed the real originality of the matter. The manuscript versions suggest rather an enquiry into the complexity of motive behind what we sum up as either a vice or a virtue. If the actual cases are examined other elements can be discerned, such as self-maintenance, physical influences, accident, temperament. His imagination has worked on his wartime experiences and all sorts of cases are brought in to test his conviction that the springs of conduct are multiple. Most of the evidence for this, within a movement like the Fronde, was of course what we should now call cynical exposure of mean motives for respectable actions. But that should not blind us to the discoveries that La Rochefoucauld made. Two discoveries above all. First, that qualities and values never function alone. We may speak of clemency, of generosity, of trickery and the like, but they are never the sole factors at work. Yet, as André Gide has said, we always tend to simplify morals, to think that a man or an act is good, or bad : 'Ce qui permet de croire à des sentiments simples c'est une façon simple de considérer les sentiments'. Nietzsche, one of La Rochefoucauld's keenest readers, was most grateful to him for this awareness of the complexity of motive.

But the second discovery was of still greater importance. It needed in the seventeenth century an effort of the imagination much greater than we can now understand to perceive conflict of motive as a principle of conduct. That age knew nothing of unconscious elements in behaviour. Its theory of conduct was cut and dried: all action was either assented to by the mind, or it was ascribed to occult and supernatural forces. 'There was then,' says Aldous Huxley, 'no hint of what we now call the subconscious mind, only the conscious self on the one hand, and on the other, God, the saints and a host of good or evil spirits. Our conception of a vast intermediate world of sub-conscious activity was unthinkable.'[1] Yet the so-called cynicism of La Rochefoucauld led him to discover more of this underworld than any contemporary seems to have done. 'La honte, la paresse et la timidité nous retiennent dans notre devoir, pendant que notre vertu en a tout l'honneur' (169). Behind this and many equally outspoken discoveries (for today most of us would accept his statement as correct) lies a restless imaginative and introspective quest that is fascinating to watch at work. The subject of his book, as he admitted in his last *maxime*, was 'la fausseté de tant de vertus apparentes'. I find no less than twenty-five of the *maximes* constructed on the same pattern, of laconic opposition of the appearance and the reality; thus, almost at random:

La gravité est un mystère du corps inventé pour cacher les défauts de l'esprit (257).

[1] *The Devils of Loudun*, p. 187.

and

La civilité est un désir d'en recevoir et d'être estimé poli (260).

Yet this is but the simplest of many patterns. The impressive thing is not the form only, but the way in which the form seems naturally, and no doubt unconsciously, married to the matter. If that matter were no more than the sour reflections of a disillusioned intriguer, it would not belong to art. It is surely time that La Rochefoucauld received the credit of being more than a formalist, of having imagined something that modern science has confirmed. For, like Balzac, he has imagined no less than he has observed. He had no clinical instruments at his disposal, other than cases of men like himself, caught up in civil war, exposed to the strain of plotting and of fighting. In these cases he discovered such diversity of motive that the only master key to fit them seemed to be a universal appetite for self preservation, a quality which he called amour propre and which modern science calls the ego. Neither term is used with the pejorative sense that some Christian morality associates with them. For La Rochefoucauld amour propre is not a vice so much as a biological factor in the human make-up. The drama of Racine at times suggests this restless demonic self. La Rochefoucauld does not suggest it: twenty years before Racine he describes it, in unsurpassed language:

Rien n'est si impétueux que ses désirs, rien de si caché que ses desseins, rien de si habile que ses conduites; ses souplesses ne se peuvent représenter, ses transformations passent celles de la métamorphose, et ses raffinements ceux de la chimie. On ne peut sonder la profondeur de ses projets, ni percer les ténèbres de ses abîmes. Là il est à couvert des yeux les plus pénétrants, il y fait mille insensibles tours et retours. . . .

At times La Rochefoucauld thinks of this subconscious part of human nature as more immediate and powerful than our rational activities. Like Pascal he calls it, for want of a better name, the heart. The early form of No. 103 is: 'On peut connaître son esprit, mais qui peut connaître son cœur?'

What matters here is not whether nor how far he has been upheld by modern science, but that he imagined so vividly things that are now the object of observation. The test of his maximes should be, not their psychological accuracy, but their ingenuity, their variety, their darting shafts of light into dark places. For all these manoeuvres the epigram, metallic, unqualified, challenging, was an inspired medium. He is allured by the connections between physical and moral. No. 44 in a first draft reads as follows:

La faiblesse de l'esprit est mal nommée; c'est en effet la faiblesse du tempérament, qui n'est autre chose qu'une impuissance d'agir et un manque de principe de vie.

This artist sees the moral life as incessant struggle; man is a besieged city, to use his own expression. The struggle is conducted against his own weakness, against outside forces. It is not affected by precept or idea. Such 'philosophy' as we may have may work when applied to past or future struggles, but the present defeats all philosophy (22). The present is always formidable (405). We live in a world of chance; our qualities are revealed by the single occasion: 'La fortune fait paraître nos vertus et nos vices, comme la lumière fait paraître les objets' (380).

This sense of the contingent world is another of his imaginative discoveries. He has a clear vision of the fact of society and of its controlling influence on behaviour. The *Maximes* sketch the anthropology in which *Le*

Misanthrope is best understood. None of us liveth unto himself. We act differently when we know we are being watched or when we are anxious to impress. Soldiers are braver in the ranks than alone, in the daylight than at night. Bright spirits need a society in which there are fools:

C'est une grande folie de vouloir être sage tout seul (231).

Un homme d'esprit serait souvent embarrassé sans la compagnie des sots (140).

These epigrams contain more truth so to speak than their lengthy explanation could convey. No. 231 for instance is not to be read as a lucky shot, as a neat view well presented. It is the ne plus ultra of statement, filed down to a single luminous opposition. Suspense, surprise, tension, all are involved in the metallic statement that it is folly to desire wisdom (up to this point the statement is nonsense) on one's own. The same technique may be studied in others (19, 49, 130).

A variant of the luminous opposition is the single restrained image. Most poetic images would not serve the purpose of the epigram, since they require length, time, exposition. La Rochefoucauld is a master of the pinpoint image, sometimes reduced to a single word, thus:

La plupart des hommes ont, comme des plantes, des propriétés cachées que le hasard fait découvrir (344).

He likens the effect of absence on passion to the wind that blows out a candle and blows up a forest fire (276). Vice is as inextricably mixed with virtue as poison in medecine. Virtues are swallowed up in self-interest as rivers in the sea. The first flush of love is as bloom on fruit. Vices are inns to which we would find ourselves returning if we took life's journey over again. Youth is the fever of reason.

A final resource of attraction in the form is seen in the masterly handling of sound effects. Assonance, alliteration, repetition, symmetry, all these are employed to keep the reader's attention on the central terms of an epigram. Often perhaps they are not consciously arranged, and the effect is the more attractive. Was it for instance a matter of intention that the long i vowel sound should be so insistent in No. 86: 'Notre défiance justifie la tromperie d'autrui'? The first form of 128 reads: 'La subtilité est une fausse délicatesse, et la délicatesse est une subtilité solide'.

Study of the epigram as La Rochefoucauld fashioned it for his own uses fills one with respect for the artifice (in the full sense) of the artist. What on a cursory reading, which is all that most of us may have given him, appear to be reflexions of little profundity and extreme polish prove on examination to be marvels of linguistic compression, and not only so. The compression seems to bear some relation to the discovery. La Rochefoucauld has devised maximes which suggest, as by sounding a single pure note, immense fields of discovery. He has chosen this form to reveal his piecemeal explorations into uncharted country. The brevity is in deliberate contrast to the sense of the unknown, as if an explorer used single markers to chart new ground. Rarely has an artist taken more trouble not to go beyond the evidence. He imagined the ways in which humans behave; he noted signs of what he imagined. But he admitted that though he discerned forces at work, the particular conjunction of those forces in any individual could not be discerned: Il est plus aisé de connaître l'homme en général que de connaître un homme en particulier (436). He imagined, and possibly magnified, the role of deception in human relations. He may have been wrong; the society he knew was by all accounts a very false society. But whether right or wrong, as an artist he gave to his conviction a magnificent expression.

Dans toutes les professions et dans tous les arts, chacun se fait une mine et un extérieur qu'il met en la place de la chose dont il veut avoir le mérite; de sorte que tout le monde n'est composé que de mines et c'est inutilement que nous travaillons à y trouver rien de réel (No. 256 in 1665 edition).

Was Sainte-Beuve thinking of this perhaps when in a final reflexion on his beloved author he wrote: 'Pour bien entendre La Rochefoucauld il faut se dire que l'amour propre dans ses replis de protée et ses métamorphoses prend parfois des formes sublimes'?[1]

It would be interesting to find traces of an influence of the *Maximes* on contemporaries but one cannot do very much more than conjecture. One remarkable artist, over thirty years younger than La Rochefoucauld, seems to have learnt something of his secret. La Bruyère is not only a great satirist, he is a master of brevity. He put his great talents at the service of defective artistic theory: 'on ne doit écrire que pour l'instruction' suggests that he thought moral improvement the aim and end of writing. But his own epigrams are mordant and he found new uses for pungent and abbreviated forms of expression. He can even make a maxime out of neglect of a maxime:

L'on se repent rarement de parler peu, très souvent de trop parler: maxime usée et triviale que tout le monde sait, et que tout le monde ne pratique pas.[2] (301).

---

[1] *Les Poisons*, No. 72.
[2] Numbers after quoted passages refer to pages in the Garnier edition, ed. G. Mongrédien, 1948.

Yet he too is fond of the brilliant paradox: 'L'homme, qui est esprit, se mène par les yeux et les oreilles' (302). And again: 'Un dévot est celui qui, sous un roi athée, serait athée' (354). But he dislikes (as said above) the 'oracular' feature of epigram, and he prefers to cultivate other forms of brevity. Flaubert admired his use of the short pithy statement. In much of La Bruyère's writing this is the unit of description, a phrase of a few words, and very often containing only a weak verb such as 'est', strung without connectives into a list. He describes a poor man thus, and his portrait would be more correctly described as an anatomy of the social look of poverty:

Phédon a les yeux creux, le teint échauffé, le corps sec et le visage maigre, il dort peu, et d'un sommeil fort léger; il est abstrait, rêveur, et il a avec de l'esprit l'air d'un stupide: il oublie de dire ce qu'il sait, ou de parler d'événements qui lui sont connus; et s'il le fait quelquefois, il s'en tire mal, il croit peser à ceux à qui il parle, il conte brièvement, mais froidement, il ne se fait pas écouter, il ne fait point rire (p. 179).

The method is most spectacular in some of the additions to the already famous book, the immense treatment of absent-mindedness in the sixth edition, for example, known as Ménalque, or the sketch of the diplomat. Albert Sorel said of this piece that 'Qui le pénètre n'a plus rien à apprendre sur la politique du temps.' He there describes the typical ambassador as 'un caméléon, un Protée' whose statements bear no relation to what he is or what he thinks, but are entirely dictated by politics. Four pages are thus composed by the successive opposition of roles: 'il est ferme et inflexible . . . ou il est facile. Une autre fois, ou il est profond et dissimulé . . . ou il est franc et ouvert . . . de même ou il est vif et grand parleur

... ou il est froid et taciturne ... Il sait parler en termes clairs et formels, il sait encore mieux parler ambigument' (pp. 245–249).

On the whole La Bruyère prefers to render visual effects. He has an eye for contour, and will express a mood in sketching a gesture, thus:

Le comédien, couché dans son carrosse, jette de la boue au visage de Corneille qui est à pied.

His peasants when they stand up are *seen* to be men. His bird-fancier dreams he is a bird: 'lui-même il est oiseau, il est huppé, il gazouille, il perche.' His *Champagne* in the course of digesting a large dinner, signs an order depriving a province of bread. Here is the social criticism that will be so common in the eighteenth century, but expressed in short stabs of pregnant vision. La Bruyère invented a new vehicle for satire in this kind of symbolical snapshot. In a few lines he makes a figure stand out memorably because sketched, rather than described. He complains that fashion changes so quickly that his subjects are transformed before they have had time to pose. The paragraph is a beautiful example of his art:

Les couleurs sont preparées, et la toile est toute prête; mais comment le fixer, cet homme inquiet, léger, inconstant, qui change de mille et mille figures? Je le peins dévot, et je crois l'avoir attrapé; mais il m'échappe et déja il est libertin. Qu'il demeure du moins dans cette mauvaise situation, et je saurai le prendre dans un point de dérèglement de cœur et d'esprit où il sera reconnaissable, mais la mode presse, il est dévot (p. 353).

The method acquires full value from the admirable variety of approach and attitude. The artist addresses his subject, pitying him, or recounts his history, or resumes an imaginary dialogue. And the satire does not exclude a touch of sentiment. This vignette was much admired by Rébelliau:[1]

Ce palais, ces meubles, ces jardins, ces belles eaux vous enchantent et vous font récrier d'une première vue sur une maison si délicieuse, et sur l'extrème bonheur du maître qui la possède. Il n'est plus; il n'en a pas joui si agréablement ni si tranquillement que vous; il n'y a jamais eu un jour serein, ni une nuit tranquille; il s'est noyé de dettes pour la porter à ce degré de beauté où elle vous ravit. Ses créanciers l'en ont chassé: il a tourné la tête, et il l'a regardée de loin une dernière fois; et il est mort de saisissement (p. 178).

These experiments in form are still experiments in brevity, in the art of saying much in few terms. La Bruyère does not forsake the *maxime*; he seems to give it a new and rather restricted scope. In his hands it expresses no profound truth, but a pungent social comment, as here: 'Dans la société c'est la raison qui plie la première', or 'Un esprit sain puise à la cour le goût de la solitude et de la retraite.' Yet both his epigrams and his pen-pictures are so striking that one wonders if the light style of the eighteenth century does not owe much to the classical artists who, like Horace, studied to be brief.

[1] La Bruyère, *Oeuvres*. Grands Ecrivains de la France, 1912. I, i. ccxxvi.

VIII

PORTRAIT OF AN AGE

At first sight it would seem that the outburst of creative energy here studied had made no contribution to the writing of history. Among the French classical artists there is at first sight no Tacitus, no Gibbon, some would say no Clarendon, no great writer in fact who set himself to describe or to explain the past. Bossuet does this, but only incidentally, in his efforts to confound the Protestants or to educate the Dauphin. The fact calls for some explanation. It is not that the ancient historians went unread. Lanson has listed a good many translations, especially in the second half of the seventeenth century. Racine thought Tacitus the greatest painter of antiquity. Nor is it that modern histories were not written. Racine again used Mézeray and Ricaut for the Turkish background of *Bajazet*. The library of Samuel Pepys contains in French Maimbourg, Souligné, Varillas, Le Vassor, and many others. But why are all these unknown names? Why should Racine, who left the theatre to become historiographer royal, have left no prose work of value in the new field?

I suppose that the basic answer is that the century was not interested in human development. It measured the thought and achievements of the past against an abstract standard of value, which it never defined, but which took no account of time and change. The whole sweep of the human story, which Voltaire, Chateaubriand, Michelet and Renan were to find so exciting, excites hardly anybody between 1600 and 1700. Rudler says in his study of the sources of *La Princesse de Clèves*:

cette création de pensée et de raison s'appuie, comme toute la psychologie du siècle, sur la croyance en l'identité de l'homme à travers les âges: elle ne suppose pas un instant une singularité d'âme, de caractères ou de passions propre au 16e siècle.

We have seen that for Pascal history was a science of memory; that there could be techniques for dealing with conflicts of evidence seems never to have crossed his mind. La Rochefoucauld, writing about 1680 a judgement on 'Les événements de ce siècle' shows this same attitude to the past: most of it does not interest him:

L'histoire, qui nous apprend ce qui arrive dans le monde, nous montre également les grands événements et les médio-cres: cette confusion d'objets nous empêche souvent de discerner avec assez d'attention les choses extraordinaires qui sont renfermées dans le cours de chaque siècle. Celui où nous vivons en a produit, à mon sens, de plus singuliers que les précédents. . . .

'Les événements de ce siècle', this was the only kind of history that La Rochefoucauld and his contemporaries found interesting, and to such a degree that they could not help writing about it. The output of memoirs is astonishing, filling an entire volume of the *Sources de l'Histoire de France au 17e siècle*. Reading in them one realises what an exciting age it was for an intelligent European to live in. An age of discovery, of invention, of great men, of surprising reversals of fortune. Valentin Conrart, whom literary history knows as a modest man behind the scenes, has a letter to Félibien in 1647 expressing passionate interest in the Sicilian revolt (of Masaniello) and adding this comment: 'Le peuple est un animal farouche qu'il n'est aisé ni de prendre ni d'éviter. Nous verrons quelle sera la fin de cette fureur qui l'a animé dans cette rencontre.' For La Rochefoucauld the century would be memorable for the sole fact that it had produced a Cromwell:

Un lieutenant d'infanterie, sans nom et sans crédit, a commencé, à l'âge de quarante cinq ans, de se faire connaître dans les désordres d'Angleterre. Il a dépossédé son roi légitime, bon, juste, doux, vaillant et libéral; il lui a fait trancher la tête par un arrêt de son parlement; il a changé la royauté en république; il a été dix ans maître de l'Angleterre, plus craint de ses voisins et plus absolu dans son pays que tous les rois qui ont regné. Il est mort paisible et en pleine possession de toute la puissance du royaume.

There are signs that one did not need the penetration of a moralist to think about things in this way. The sense that anything might happen, that all was possible, is deep in seventeenth century life, in France as in England and Germany. Our history books have done us no service picturing Germany as racked with dissension, England as in the grip of fanatics and France calm and stable under benevolent monarchy. The very establishment of the French monarchy was a 'tentative révolutionnaire' as Sagnac has said. Stability and calm were not the dominant notes of French life, even after 1660, but (to quote

Sagnac once more): 'une activité intense, partout l'indé-
pendance de l'esprit, la bataille des idées, l'héroïsme de
l'action et de la pensée.'[2]

This uncertainty came to a head in the Fronde and is
reflected in the mass of pamphlets and memoirs which
civil war inspired. I think that its repercussions extend
later into the century than is often said, that its partici-
pants always felt themselves suspect to the King and his
ministers, that Louis' attitude to Jansenism and Protestantism was coloured by his continuing fears of insubor-
dination. The feeling of tension, the lack of stability
encouraged the writing of memoirs to justify one's role,
to refute rumour and calumny, or simply to tell an
exciting tale. It is impossible to read this mass of literature
and continue to think of French society as conformist
or dull or modelled on a single pattern. Such an author
as Tallemant des Réaux for example shows, in his own
person no less than in his indefatigable note-taking, the
restless activity of which Sagnac has written. Our point
here is that this has affected the literature, which we may
call classical; this brings us round again to the heart
of the subject. This mass of memoirs produced many
interesting writers, and three at least who may be called
great. Their works have been constantly reprinted, and
have influenced later writers. None of them wished to
write a history of their times. One of them is famous for a
private correspondence. Another wrote to justify his part
in the 'troubles'. A third, born out of time as it were in
1679, only prepared his work for publication after 1740.
Yet in some degree all share the same point of view; all
describe the same society. One is acknowledged a
'classical' writer; the others are not. It is as difficult to

[2] P. Sagnac, op. cit. p. 23.

account for the inclusion of the one as for the exclusion of the others, unless we admit that the traditional categories are too narrow and artificial.

Taken together the writings of Mme de Sévigné, Retz and Saint-Simon constitute a body of literature as impressive as anything mentioned in this essay. To the communication of the 'form and body' of their time, they brought a mastery of language, a range of experience and a power of imagination that may well not be history as now understood, but that it is difficult not to call great literature. They confirm the impression, suggested by the work of Pascal and La Rochefoucauld and Bossuet, that the finest French classical literature is incidental, not in the first place written for the public. There is no need to dwell here on the usual and much commented features of Mme de Sévigné's letters. The attraction of her writing lies chiefly in her skill in conveying both the variety and the dramatic interest of upper-class French life, one might say of the larger court circle. She is no revolutionary: she sees people and things with the eyes of a French aristocrat and monarchist. The least word from the King is for her a great experience. Her limitations remind one of those of a parallel figure, Jane Austen. She has a critical mind, but no thought of criticising the structure of society, the administration of justice, the decision to make war or peace. The people she considers in the mass ('cette immensité de Bretons'). She judges the taxpayers of Provence without any understanding of their case. They should be thankful that her son-in-law (and their Governor, M. de Grignan) stood well with the King; 'sans lui ils auraient senti ce que c'est de ne pas obéir aveuglément. Le Languedoc n'a fait aucune difficulté de donner ce que le Roi a demandé . . . la Bretagne donne plus qu'on ne veut . . . il n'y a que cette petite Provence.'[3] She is emotional but not at all Romantic, and would not have understood Rousseau's plea for the individual. Yet she is an individual, with immediate reactions, and affections. She has, and is conscious of it, her own way of putting things.

Her vivacity of impression is extreme, in reporting a conversation, in judging a play, in describing a trial. She is an excellent reporter, and more than a reporter. Only a writer of imagination could have grasped, and rendered, the peculiar pleasure given by a court performance of *Esther*:

c'est un rapport de la musique, des vers, des chants, des personnes, si parfait et si complet qu'on n'y souhaite rien . . . on est attentif et on n'a point d'autre peine que celle de voir finir une si agréable pièce . . . tous les chants, convenables aux paroles et mis dans le sujet, sont d'une beauté qu'on ne soutient pas sans larmes: la mesure de l'approbation qu'on donne à cette pièce est celle du goût et de l'attention.

This imaginative perception is frequent in her letters, sometimes in a single phrase as when she reports the death of Louvois, 'lui qui était le centre de tant de choses'. Marcel Proust, one of her devoted readers, compared her with Dostoievski for her reporting of details as they strike the eye, the macabre on a level with the insignificant thus at the end of a letter:

J'étais dans une petite allée, à main gauche du mail, très obscure; je la trouvai belle: je fis écrire sur un arbre: E di mezzo l'horrore esce il diletto.

This writer is an *immediate* person. Her reading is a part of her, like her seeing and speaking. It is eclectic: Nicole

[3] Ed. Pléiade, I. 443.

and Tasso, Abbadie and Pascal, La Fontaine, and Corneille. She quotes Racine's *Alexandre* and Quinault's *Thésée* as easily as she quotes La Fontaine and Molière. She knows her Ganelon as she knows her Don Quixote. She finds some of the *Maximes* 'divines'. 'Despréaux vous ravira par ses vers' she writes after hearing l'*Art Poétique* read in a salon. The long series of letters to one person might well have proved monotonous for others to read, yet this seems never to happen. Nor does she seem consciously to avoid monotony. The expression is always unexpected, spontaneous and yet always controlled. The famous letter to Coulanges in 1670 beginning 'Je m'en vais vous mander la chose la plus étonnante' and delaying the news to the end of the letter, is a masterpiece of suspense and playful dialogue. Since nothing is heavy, nor of prescribed length and form, the transitions are easy; we pass from news to domesticity, from grave to gay, from gossip to religion. The quality of the writing appears in these transitions; one may note how she gives rein to reflexion, pursuing a point as if curious to see what it will make her say, and the reader finds that he has been given a glimpse into an essential element of the human condition, but without fuss or parade. Here is a page which many will want to call classical art, on a level of expression with Racine's *Bajazet* announced in the same letter. Let us not talk of Freudian introspection, but neither let us think that the seventeenth century faced a world less problematic than our own:[4]

Vous me demandez, ma chère enfant, si j'aime toujours bien la vie. Je vous avoue que j'y trouve des chagrins cuisants; mais je suis encore plus dégoutée de la mort: je me trouve si malheureuse d'avoir à finir tout ceci par elle, que si je

[4] Ed. Pléiade, I. 497.

pouvais retourner en arrière, je ne demanderais pas mieux.
Je me trouve dans un engagement qui m'embarrasse; je suis
embarquée dans la vie sans mon consentement; il faut que
j'en sorte, cela m'assomme. Et comment en sortirai-je? Par
où? Par quelle porte? Quand sera-ce? En quelle disposition?
Souffrirai-je mille et mille douleurs, qui me feront mourir
désespérée? Aurai-je un transport au cerveau? Mourrai-je
d'un accident? Comment serai-je avec Dieu? Qu'aurai-je à lui
présenter? La crainte, la nécessité, feront-elles mon retour
vers lui? N'aurai-je aucun autre sentiment que celui de la peur?
Que puis-je espérer? Suis-je digne du paradis? Suis-je digne
de l'enfer? Quelle alternative. Quel embarras. Rien n'est si fou
que de mettre son salut dans l'incertitude; mais rien n'est si
naturel, et la sotte vie que je mène est la chose du monde la
plus aisée à comprendre. Je m'abîme dans ces pensées et je
trouve la mort si terrible que je hais plus la vie parce qu'elle
m'y mène, que par les épines qui s'y rencontrent. Vous me
direz que je veux vivre éternellement. Point du tout; mais si
on m'avait demandé mon avis, j'aurais bien aimer à mourir
entre les bras de ma nourrice; cela m'aurait ôté bien des ennuis
et m'aurait donné le ciel bien sûrement et bien aisément; mais
parlons d'autre chose. . . .

The fact that the author of this passage had an affection
for the Cardinal de Retz and probably induced him to put
his adventures on paper should make us grateful to her
and respectful to him. It seems that in later life he was not
the turncoat and the unstable main-chancer whom
historians of the Fronde depict. His great work prepared
the way for a view of history which he did not himself
hold: Gibbon read him closely. It is, as Sainte-Beuve said,
a breviary of revolution, a presentation of one man's
part in the Fronde; the very qualities which make it
unreliable as history show the workings of an imaginative
and critical mind, able to recreate the sense of a complex

situation, and to use its complexity in attempting a better judgement of men.

We do not know whether Retz was suiting the facts to his vanity when he said that his first work had attracted the attention of Richelieu, but we do know what that work was: it contains the germ of his whole political attitude. It was a re-writing of Mascardi's account of the conspiracy of Count Fieschi against the government of Genoa. Retz contrives to repeat the facts and to present the main actor as a great man rather than as a criminal. The stigma of conspiracy is removed: we follow the story of 'une grande entreprise' which, had it met with success, would have placed its author among the heroes of the age; 'tant il est vrai que le bon ou mauvais événement est la règle ordinaire des louanges ou du blâme que l'on donne aux actions extraordinaires.'

Here is a first sketch of Retz' distinctive contribution to historical writing. He is a student of Machiavelli and a cool analyst of politics. He insists that the very different realms of thought and of action should not be judged by the same criteria. Action has taught him the existence of, and inspired him with admiration for, a new morality, which he is fascinated to recall, and we to read. This is existential writing, concerned with the forces involved in the management of men and the use of power. To handle men is itself a great thing, and not always possible by moral means: 'Y a-t-il une action plus grande au monde que la conduite d'un parti? Celle d'une armée a sans comparaison moins de ressorts, celle d'un Etat en a davantage; mais les ressorts n'en sont à beaucoup près ni si fragiles ni si délicats . . . .' And again: 'L'on ne connaît pas ce qu'est le parti quand on s'imagine que le chef en est le maître.'

Reading such passages suggests that the experiences of the Fronde had their importance for French outlook as well as for the French State. They allowed a clear-sighted observer to discover a new criterion of action, a new morality, that made him sceptical of the more traditional morality of the philosophers. The frontispiece of the *Maximes*, showing a sprite tearing off the mask of Seneca, might have served for Retz' *Mémoires*.

The Cardinal is not afraid to take his own case as an example of what must have seemed criminal deception. He shows how respect for the church enabled a church-man to utilise the supernatural as a means of dominating the crowd. Admitting that he was 'l'âme peut-être la moins ecclésiastique qui fût dans l'univers' he is led to reflect on the pitfalls which beset the cleric in public life:

il n'y a rien qui soit si sujet à l'illusion que la piété. Toutes sortes d'erreurs se glissent et se cachent sous son voile; elle consacre toutes sortes d'imaginations, et la meilleure intention ne suffit pas pour y faire éviter les travers. . . . Les affaires brouillent les espèces, elles honorent même ce qu'elles ne justifient pas; et les vices d'un archevêque peuvent être en une infinité de rencontres les vertus d'un chef de parti.

The disillusionment is complete. We feel we are looking at human nature afresh. As Sainte-Beuve puts it: 'il n'est rien de tel que de voir une Fronde pour se rafraîchir dans l'idée de la nature humaine. On a beau être né marin, il n'est rien de tel que de voir une tempête . . . .'[5] One wonders if the Libertin thinkers have not had too much credit for the advance of incredulity in the eighteenth century. Such writing as this must have been of great effect.

[5] *Nouveaux Lundis*, iii. 230.

Like La Rochefoucauld Retz is led by the life of intrigue and conspiracy to study particular cases. He chides Molé for not doing just this: 'il jugeait toujours les actions par les hommes et presque jamais les hommes par les actions.'[6] He studies the factors within and beyond human control, timing for instance: 'Il n'y a rien dans le monde qui n'ait son moment décisif et le chef-d'œuvre de la bonne conduite est de connaître et de prendre ce moment'. Time, and reversal of fortune, turn advice into crime: 'Les avis qu'on donne (aux ministres) passent pour des crimes toutes les fois qu'on ne leur est pas agréable.' Action in fact is mysterious, and is the realm of the unexpected. Like Pomponne between his various embassies, Retz is bored by inaction and loves to recall the thrills of a perilous existence. He writes like a showman suiting his surprises to his public: 'Vous allez voir des scènes au prix desquelles les passées n'ont été que des verdures et des pastourelles'. This is not altogether bravado. Revolution brings out the hidden motives and instincts behind civility. Fear for example:

Je n'ai jamais vu à la comédie italienne de peur si naivement et si ridiculement représentée que celle qu'il fit voir à la Reine.

Some passages in Retz seem arranged on a similar principle to scenes in Molière. In both authors we watch characters playing parts and being driven from their part by pressure of the game:

La vérité est que tout ce qui était dans ce cabinet jouait la comédie: je faisais l'innocent et je ne l'étais pas . . . le Cardinal faisait l'assuré . . . la Reine contrefit la douce . . . jamais plus aigre. M. le Duc d'Orléans faisait l'empressé.[7]

[6] Ed. Pléiade, p. 157.
[7] Pléiade, p. 87.

'Les choses cachées,' he remarked later in a pamphlet, 'sont proprement le champ de l'imposture.'

Retz and La Rochefoucauld were once persuaded to draw up a portrait of each other. Political enemies, they were in fact kindred spirits; they analyse conduct in much the same way, and reach similar conclusions. Both were reluctant to pronounce on a particular case, knowing that action might have various explanations. La Rochefoucauld as we have seen wrote that 'Il est plus aisé de connaître l'homme en général que de connaître un homme en particulier' (No. 436). Retz took the same thought into the field of historical writing: 'It is not to be wondered at that writers treating of matters in which they were not themselves concerned should be so frequently wrong, since even those closest to the event cannot avoid, in cases without number, mistaking for reality appearances that are often false in every detail.' Did Fontenelle read this passage before writing his reflexions on the Golden Tooth? Retz lacks the imaginative power to visualise the protean ego, but in some ways he is more daring than La Rochefoucauld. To read him is to absorb a mood singularly free from traditional conceptions of morality. Long before Nietzsche and the Marxists he described the will to power, the 'Umwertung aller Werte', the sort of situation in which all means are permitted provided the end be worth the scandal that the means will provoke.

The latest editor of Retz finds in him 'des scènes rendues avec une acuité psychologique qui les égale à Saint-Simon'. Retz might well have desired no greater compliment than comparison with the famous duke about whom the literary histories are so shy, but who is now recognised among the great French masters of language.

The society which Retz observed in travail of birth, Saint-Simon observes in full formal splendour. The notes that he started to take in 1694, and which he continued to perfect for nearly fifty years, are outwardly a record of personalities, but really an analysis sharpened by mistrust of the King's power, the strain of war, the conflicts of politicians and of great ladies. The argument would have been pulverised by Retz, who had an acute sense of realities and was bound to no theory, but it proceeds with massive evidence and imposing momentum as an indictment of the betrayal of the aristocracy, of a 'règne de vile bourgeoisie' during which a King who was famous, but who should have known better, allowed power to slip into the hands of clerks and middle class men without regard for traditional values.

It is a book, almost a library, of which only a part has been published, full of prejudice and of great imaginative power. With all the power of a poet, this writer treats what is a favourite seventeenth-century theme, the eternal contrast between nature and behaviour. We are shown the great of the earth in all their parade and pomp, yet engaged and enmeshed in a life of passion and intrigue and vicious deceit. We never read of the appearance without suggestion of the reality behind and beneath. The polished manners are shown up by the savage instincts, the grand dignity by the petty plotting. Did Marx ever read this indictment of a society needing money, wasting money, hardly conscious of the power of money, thoughtless in its use of money? The ravages of pride in Racine, the fall of the proud in Molière, the judgement of pride in La Rochefoucauld and La Bruyère, all these emphases are here in a new and larger context. Yet the detail does not tire us. We rather get from this endless procession the feeling that Shakespeare and Balzac convey, a long search for the human case that may stand for full humanity, a conjunction of opposites so clear as to suggest the full circle of human nature.

He passes so many courtiers for instance in review that he seems to be testing one specimen after another in the effort to find out what goes to the making of the type: the fund of capacity, the layer of manners, the dynamo of self-interest, he shows us all these at work, again and again. He finds what he wants in the two Harlays, lawyer and churchman. His picture of the former is in three parts: the general judgement that one would expect at the end comes first, then a double list of talents and vices, then a picture of what the man looked like, a picture in which, again as in Balzac, the physical features seem to enforce the moral qualities we have been told about. The whole thing is presented at speed, as a *raccourci*. Saint-Simon constantly tells us how much he has left out, how much could be said: 'On ferait un volume de ses traits, d'autant plus perçants qu'il avait infiniment d'esprit.' Here is the judgement:

Issu de ces grands magistrats, Harlay en eut toute la gravité, qu'il outragea en cynique, en affecta le désintéressement et la modestie, qu'il déshonora, l'une par sa conduite, l'autre par un orgueil raffiné mais extrême et qui malgré lui sautait aux yeux. Il se piqua surtout de probité et de justice, dont le masque tomba bientôt. Entre Pierre et Jacques il conservait la plus exacte droiture, mais dès qu'il apercevait un intérêt ou une faveur à ménager, tout aussitôt il était vendu . . . .

Not far away is a companion piece in the sketch of the archbishop, seen in his decline, which Saint-Simon attributes to the antipathy of Mme de Maintenon:

Cet esprit étendu, juste, solide et toutefois fleuri, qui pour la partie du gouvernement en faisait un grand évêque et pour celle du monde un grand seigneur fort aimable et un courtisan parfait, quoique fort noblement, ne put s'accoutumer à cette décadence, et au discrédit qui l'accompagna. Le clergé, qui s'en aperçut et à qui l'envie n'est pas étrangère, se plut à se venger de sa domination, quoique douce et polie, qu'il en avait éprouvée, et lui résista, pour le plaisir de l'oser et de le pouvoir. Le monde, qui n'a eu plus besoin de lui pour des évêchés et des abbayes, l'abandonna. Toutes les grâces de son corps et de son esprit, qui étaient infinies, et qui lui étaient parfaitement naturelles, se flétrirent. Il ne se trouva de ressources qu'à se renfermer avec sa bonne amie la duchesse de Lesdiguières, qu'il voyait tous les jours de sa vie, ou chez elle ou à Conflans, dont il avait fait un jardin délicieux, et qu'il tenait si propre qu'à mesure qu'ils s'y promenaient tous deux, des jardiniers les suivaient à distance, pour effacer leurs pas avec des rateaux.

This is surely an imaginative portrait of great skill, and it could be illustrated from a thousand such silhouettes.

The accuracy of each portrait is not here our concern, and has been matter of conjecture ever since Sainte-Beuve reacted to the findings of M. Chéruel in 1865. The truth which Saint-Simon gives is probably not that of history, but it is the truth of art. It is a picture of what the human organism can be, and endure, and achieve, based no doubt on fact, but 'going beyond the evidence' as E. M. Forster says the novelist must do, into the realm of suggestion. Saint-Simon's power of suggestion concerning personality is almost infinite. What we are dealing with is description at the service of passion, which seems to lend wings to the style. Resentment at the new civil service will burst out in a rhetorical relative clause: 'Le superbe du Roi, qui forme le *colosse* de ses ministres sur la *ruine* de la noblesse.' Details, as if held in reserve, suddenly flood the page and create an overwhelming impression. It is not the accuracy of fact stored by observation: imagination has been animating the memory of things seen. Listen to this 'historian' on the ignorance of Louis XIV:

Sa dépendance fut extrême. A peine lui apprit-on à lire et à écrire; il demeura tellement ignorant que les choses les plus connues d'histoire, d'événements, de fortunes, de conduites, de naissance, de lois, il n'en sut jamais un mot. Il tomba par ce défaut et quelquefois en public dans les absurdités les plus grossières. . . .

If one seeks for a principle of composition, the most obvious feature is the apparent absence of selection. In classical drama, poetry, and even in the longest novel, the author treats a chosen and limited subject, chosen with a view to the effect intended. In letters and memoirs this would not seem to be so. The impression of dealing with the haphazard is much greater. I think with Auerbach that serious study of Saint-Simon must start at this point. Discussing the material that has gone into the *Mémoires* he says: 'Saint-Simon does not invent, he works with the random unselected material which life presents to him.'[8] So we have an artist of great power, sharing the outlook of the classical writers we have been considering, looking at the same society as they looked at, yet who does not, like La Bruyère, describe its aberrations, its freaks, its disregard of morality, but makes all these aspects incidental to a picture of how the great behave, in peace and war, in joy and grief, in passion and in control. Not many artists have set themselves a larger canvas. One may at

[8] *Mimesis*, p. 416.

times feel lost, or even that the author is swamped by his matter, but the compensations are great, and the artistic effects are tremendous, as Mr. Auerbach has noted: 'The non-fictitious, non-precogitated quality of his material . . . gives Saint-Simon a depth of life which even Molière or La Bruyère could not achieve.'

The material may be unselected, but it is not un-arranged. The author has a plan and a scheme of pres-entation. He groups his materials under personalities introduced chronologically at the time of a person's death. This allows him to write as it were a court diary of the last thirty years of the reign, and to be at all times free to revert to what has happened earlier. The story of Lauzun for instance, is told with other events of the year of his death, 1723. The larger blocks of material have separate chapters: Crayon du Duc d'Orléans, Caractère de Louis XIV, Les Amours du Roi, Madame de Maintenon, etc. Within each section the sequence is logical: general fea-tures, particular issues, resumé and judgement. In this vast number of pages no fact seems unrelated, as if put in for record only, always for evidence. This is a feature of the whole work: we are not given history or fact, so much as evidence building up a case. It is not an account of a régime so much as an indictment, to which all the details contribute. At some point they are accumulated, summarised and evaluated, usually in some eloquent apostrophe 'Voilà où conduisit . . . ' or 'C'est là ce qui fit . . . .'

Saint-Simon gave some thought to his method, as we see from a passage on repetition:

Je me trouve, je l'avoue, entre la crainte de quelques redites et celle de ne pas expliquer assez en détail des curio-sités que nous regrettons dans toutes les Histoires et dans presque toutes les Mémoires des divers temps. On voudrait y voir les princes, avec leurs maîtresses et leurs ministres, dans leur vie journalière. . . . C'est ce qui m'enhardit sur l'inconvénient des redites. Tout bien considéré j'estime qu'il vaut mieux hasarder qu'il m'en échappe quelques-unes que ne pas mettre sous les yeux un tout ensemble si intéressant.[9]

Complexity and fullness of detail are not the only ingredients. Saint-Simon is a master of summary, or of luminous abbreviation of what he is about to recount in detail. Even the style uses with great effect the collective neuter: 'tout ce qui était dans Marly', or 'le peu de courtisans considérables qui s'y présentèrent'. Even more effective perhaps thus: 'Il s'appelait Rémond et frappait à tout ce qui se trouvait de portes'.[1] The end of the king's life, ten pages of minute chronological reporting, is introduced by the quarrel among the doctors that made the best advice impossible. Fagon, King's physician, though of advanced years, had such a reputation that he would brook no second opinion: 'Il ne voulait ni raisons ni réplique, et continuait de conduire la santé du Roi comme il avait fait dans un âge moins avancé, et le tua par cette opiniâtreté.' So the account we are about to read is not left in the air, as it were. It is the story of how Fagon killed the King. After all is over, comes the judgement on life and character: 'Ce fut un prince à qui on ne peut refuser beaucoup de bon . . . .'

The unique quality of Saint-Simon's writing is due in great part to the use of two deliberate devices: he has gone outside the usual sources of information, and he has overstepped the conventional bounds of language. His passion for getting to what really happened, especially if

[9] G. E. xxviii. 276.
[1] Pl´iade, v. 157.

it fit in with his suspicions, leads him to welcome the unscrupulous or the unreliable source wherever it is picturesque. We cannot control his authorities; he may in many cases not have been able to do so. After a breathless page describing how the King took the fire tongs to attack Louvois, Boislisle comments: 'De qui Saint-Simon peut-il tenir sur la conduite intime du ministre des détails si précis, qu'il est absolument seul à rapporter?'[2] The answer is probably a valet, or a gossip. The details about Louis' death he got from Maréchal, a surgeon in attendance on Fagon. Occasionally the control of the artist slips and we get a story put in because he cannot bring himself to leave it untold. Thus in the account of Monsieur: 'Je ne puis finir sur ce Prince sans raconter une anecdote qui a été sue de bien peu de gens sur la mort de Madame'.

Even more striking is the admission into his pages, by this stickler for etiquette, of unconventional and indecent language. If the ugly, as Boileau said, has to be transformed in order to become material of art, then Saint-Simon is not of the school of Boileau. But in prose, all the classical artists use the physical expression that would be banned from the salon and from poetry. But none with such frequency and such force as Saint-Simon. No details seem to him taboo if they bring the reality before us, and that reality is often physical. So in describing the illness of the Dauphin he notes the 'évacuation prodigieuse haut et bas'. Auerbach has analysed the wonderful vignettes of the Duchesse de Bourgogne taking an enema in the King's presence, and of the Duc d'Orléans on his stool. Neither detail is irrelevant: the point could not be made without them. Of the latter case, Auerbach comments:

[2] G. E. xxviii. 69, n.

The point is not simply that we have here a ruthless representation of every-day events, of things that are ugly, and in terms of classical aesthetics undignified. . . . The point is rather that these things are made to serve a completely serious character portrayal which explores the problematic and even transcends the purely moralistic in order to penetrate into the 'profondeurs opaques' of our nature. . . Saint-Simon is a precursor of modern and ultra-modern forms of conceiving and representing life.[3]

Some of these descriptions beat La Bruyère at his own game. The subject is reduced to moral insignificance under adverse physical detail. Thus Monsieur:

C'était un petit homme ventru, monté sur des échasses tant ses souliers étaient hauts, toujours paré comme une femme, plein de bagues, de bracelets, de pierreries partout . . . des rubans partout où il en pouvait mettre . . . on l'accusait de mettre imperceptiblement du rouge.

The description of this man's brother seems violent to the point of indecency. Saint-Simon is not concerned with convention. He is determined to enforce the contrast of the King's excessive politeness and his tyrannical demands of punctuality regardless of any consideration for ladies:

C'était un homme uniquement personnel, et qui ne comptait tous les autres, quels qu'ils fussent, que par rapport à soi. Sa dureté là-dessus était extrême. Dans les temps les plus vifs de sa vie pour ses maîtresses, leurs incommodités les plus opposées aux voyages et au grand habit de cour . . . rien ne pouvait les en dispenser. Grosses, malades, moins de six semaines après leurs couches, en d'autres temps fâcheux, il fallait être en grand habit, parées et serrées dans leur corps, aller en Flandres et plus loin encore, danser, veiller, être des fêtes, . . . et tout cela precisément aux jours et aux heures marquées, sans déranger

[3] Ibid. p. 431.

rien d'une minute . . . Avec cela, d'aucuns besoins il n'en fallait
point parler. . . . La Duchesse de Chevreuse s'est soulagée
pleinement dans la chapelle de Fontainebleau.[4]

More shocking to a modern reader is the violence of
expression that goes along with this ruthless attempt to
convey the force and fibre of things. No scorn is too bad
for Mme de Maintenon 'la sultane manquée' or for the
King's bastard children, 'la boue infecte du double
adultère'. The contrast must be complete. It is that of
Pascal's angel and beast, but rendered lavishly and
savagely instead of succinctly. These grand people are
lords and ladies, but they are human organisms as well.
They have grand designs, and mean minds; their dignity
is imposing, but it breaks down. The finest passages here
again concern the King himself, whose politeness surprises us as it does the historian:

Jamais homme si naturellement poli, ni d'une politesse si
fort mesurée, si fort par degrés, ni qui distinguât mieux l'âge,
le mérite, le rang, et dans ses réponses, quand elles passaient
le *je verrai*, et dans ses manières. Ces étages divers se marquaient
exactement dans sa manière de saluer et de recevoir les révé-
rences, lorsqu'on partait ou qu'on arrivait. Il était admirable à
recevoir différemment les saluts à la tête des lignes à l'armée ou
aux revues. Mais surtout pour les femmes rien n'était pareil.
Jamais il n'a passé devant la moindre coiffe sans soulever son
chapeau, je dis aux femmes de chambre, et qu'il connaissait
pour telles, comme cela arrivait souvent à Marly.

This and much more to the same effect increases the
interest of those occasions when even for him the strain
was too great. I only know of two when he lost his temper, once with a valet to whom he used his cane, once

[4] G. E. xxviii. 266.

when Louvois to test him said that he had sent off the order to burn Treves:

Le Roi fut à l'instant, et contre son naturel, si transporté de colère, qu'il se jeta sur les pincettes de la cheminée, et en allait charger Louvois sans Mme de Maintenon, qui se jeta aussitôt entre deux, en s'écriant: Ah, Sire, qu'allez-vous faire?' et lui ôta les pincettes des mains, Louvois cependant gagnait la porte. Le Roi cria après lui pour le rappeler et lui dit les yeux étincelants: Dépêchez un courrier tout à cette heure avec un contre-ordre, et qu'il arrive à temps, et sachez que votre tête en répond, si on brûle une seule maison'. Louvois, plus mort que vif, s'en alla sur-le-champ.[5]

The same care works up the full contrast in the account of ceremonies and buildings, the luxury alongside the ugliness and the cramped conditions. The account of Versailles is well known; that of Marly is even more brilliant. This 'little place' designed to be modest and cheap which in the end involved fountains and cascades and the removal and replanting of forests, the whole account, as it were, is added up and then, as if to relieve his, and our, feelings, Saint-Simon deals the hammer-blow conclusion:

Telle fut la fortune d'un repaire de serpents et de charognes, de crapauds et de grenouilles, uniquement choisi pour n'y pouvoir dépenser.

He communicates to his reader the desire for space to repeat his virtuoso performances at due length. Here one can only say that the use of all the devices of style does allow the emergence, all the more impressive for being apparently unsought, of what Auerbach has called 'sudden descents into the depths of human existence'. One single terrific paragraph accumulates eleven reasons why the rule of the most flattered of monarchs ended in military and social disaster; eloquent in itself, this imposing catalogue is not the last word; the judgement of the partial historian attempts to convey something of the terror of the judgement to come:

Conduit ainsi jusqu'au dernier bord du précipice, avec l'horrible loisir d'en reconnaître toute la profondeur, la toute puissante main qui n'a posé que quelques grains de sable pour bornes aux plus furieux orages de la mer, arrêta tout d'un coup la dernière ruine de ce roi si présomptueux et si superbe, après lui avoir fait goûter à longs traits sa faiblesse, sa misère, son néant.[6]

These magnificent accents seem to me to be the last echoes of the great movement of verbal expression granted to the splendid century, so like its concrete glories in dignity and elevation that it is no wonder perhaps that scholars have tried to explain the one by the other. But though written in mid-eighteenth century, and read only in the nineteenth, the origin and true habitat of this style is the age in which Boileau and La Bruyère defined, and many of their contemporaries practised, that quality of style which they called 'le sublime'.

[6] Ibid. xxviii. 98.

IX

THE
SHAPE OF AN ATTITUDE

To any who have been able to read the preceding pages without exasperation there is not much more to say. I have tried to look afresh at the works of French literature usually known as classical, and to suggest that in the light of modern research they do not fit the categories to which they are by tradition assigned. To suggest new categories, and a new definition of 'classical', may well be premature, and beyond my scope. Certain enquiries into the nature of artistic creation need to be undertaken before profitable reassessment becomes possible. But there is no longer need to allow the framework to determine our way of looking at the picture in the frame. Study of the actual works may lead us to take up again Faguet's phrase 'c'est l'esprit du 17e siècle que nous appelons proprement l'esprit classique français'. The works here discussed are inspired by an outlook that cannot be called 'Renaissance', nor 'Enlightenment', and which seems to show the values accepted most fully in the late seventeenth century. But we should not forget that we partly know what those values are from the literature to which we are now applying the values. This is why judgements of literature are apt to be so tricky and misleading.

The old picture of French classicism was certainly convenient. The French are fond of theory, and such exponents as Chapelain and Boileau seemed to be defining the best writing of their age. The strain of reason and clarity running through the literature made it easy to describe as cartesian. The strain of satire and critical analysis in the same literature gave point to Faguet's suggestion that it was inspired by 'un génie critique admirablement délié et fin, peu créateur.' Finally the element of elegance and dignity, and the close association of writers with the Court, suggested a common spirit animating both.

All this was very convenient, and procrustean. The works came to be increasingly looked at as illustrations of the explanation. Other features were played down. The eighteenth century (to take but one case) had so enforced the notion of the *Art Poétique* as an imposed code of writing that even such a scholar as Curtius continued (in 1946) to call Boileau a schoolmaster, unable to appreciate real poetry. Research has ruined the structure, point by point. Not only Boileau, but Corneille, Pascal, Molière, Mlle de Scudéry, Descartes, all these have been shown to be less universal, abstract, impersonal, than they were once thought. The temptation is great to adopt the opposite explanations: to call these works baroque and not classical, to say Racine is a personal and subjective author, that the so-called 'classical' psychology is not so deep, or that preciosity was nothing but a party cry. On all these points of course there is room for disagreement.

If we discard the clichés, and look at the major works as we have tried here to do, what do we actually find? A short answer would be that we find certain writers of great power, who would no doubt have been surprised to be told that they were engaged in communicating the same general attitude. We find also, as a common factor in the reception of their works, a discerning public, which liked many forms of writing, from the most fantastic to the most prosaic, but which welcomed the new drama, in its severest form, which in the salons encouraged the epigram and applauded Boileau and La Fontaine, and which in 1688 was numerous enough to buy four editions of *Les Caractères* in a few months. A small public no doubt, but one which appreciated what the King himself called 'esprit' and what Racine called 'raisonnable', a public which encouraged Corneille and Molière, again not exclusively, but clearly enough to indicate appreciation of what they were doing. And what were they doing? Seen in retrospect, they were for one thing creating a new type of drama. They were creating plays in which were rhythmically presented conflicts inherent in civilised life, not stories nor clever plots so much as basic confrontations of violent qualities. These conflicts implied heroic attitudes that were yet recognisably contemporary: the soldier, the martyr, the general, and so on. They showed such people confronted by the limits of their power, by the forces of state or church or family.

The dramatist who after the Fronde best uses this new form shows men in similar conflicts, more often conquered than conquering: 'Errante et sans dessein je cours dans ce palais.' Why does the poet imagine a princess so distracted? Not because any wild adventure had happened, but because he wished to show a person torn by the conflict of love and pride, a condition he was several times to put in dramatic form. Is it an accident that a brilliant writer of epigram should independently be imagining similar situations? 'La table des matières des déguisements de l'amour-propre selon La Rochefoucauld se confond avec la liste des vertus chevaleresques . . . le grandissement héroïque de l'image humaine, la puissance souveraine du moi, la hauteur des désirs sont en cause dans les *Maximes*,' says a recent scholar.[1]

This same critique of human behaviour may be found in the notes of Pascal and the comedy of Molière. It seems inseparable from a vivid sense of human achievement, accompanied by an equally lively sense of the limitations imposed on action either by human nature or by non-human forces, or by society. In both writers there is more than critical analysis; there is a power of imagination that can express the results of analysis in unforgettable form. Molière seems at times to reach the artistic *ne plus ultra* of play acting. In the various puppets that he not only conceived but often also played, he acts the part of modern man acting a part, of entrepreneur, of crook, of stoic or cynic. The attitudes of pride, of authority, of learning, of self-importance, are all shown up as false, in so far as they have neglected even more basic human forces: they are not, as their subjects thought, the real man, not the whole man, but in their defeat they suggest the human situation, with its conflicts of reason and will, of individual and society. No definition of classicism so far devised has perhaps done justice to this imaginative power of Molière, which does not seem different in kind from the power of Pascal in *Les Provinciales*, of Bossuet

1 P. Bénichou, *Morales du grand siècle*, 1948, p. 110.

in his orations, or of La Bruyère in his mordant vignettes.

It would seem then that in several writers, and in very different kinds of writing, we meet a common attitude. The similarity may be discerned by any careful reader. Had we read no books about books would we not say that the novelist who imagined the dilemma of the princesse de Clèves was a contemporary of Racine and Pascal? That Pascal's thoughts on politics came out of experiences similar to those of Retz and La Rochefoucauld? The elements common to such vivid pictures would seem to be intellectual penetration and a certain tradition of hierarchical values, not in themselves ever discussed but which offer a basis on which the imagined conflicts might take shape. If man be not autonomous, if the world be not clear evidence of a creator, if indeed the Christian values be not assumed, then surely such books as *Dom Juan*, *Les Caractères*, *La Princesse de Clèves* and *Phèdre* lose their meaning, since all these works show cases of revolt or refusal of what it is assumed normal to accept.

Let us look further at the common features of the works we have in these pages been discussing. Have they not a common attitude to language, a common acceptance of elegance and dignity, a common refusal of vulgarity and individual idiosyncrasy? Not only so, but a common respect for form, that is, of a casting of the material into a form, determined not by any outside authority but by the demands of that material. If this be so (as I suspect) then the meaning of their works is given partly by the form: what each of them says cannot be discerned apart from the way in which it is said. Furthermore it is truly respect: the traditional forms such as drama and epigram and satire and fable are not lightly cast aside.

The subject matter too of most of these works is such as one would find in the seventeenth century, not before or since. Summarised, the general theme is the emotional behaviour of civilised people, but this behaviour is seen in its conflicts and oppositions: of head and heart, of self and society. The cases analysed are those that bring out the basic qualities, the hidden qualities, those that we strive to hide or do not acknowledge, as the complement to the qualities of parade and public display. In a word these works all suggest in their own way a true vision of human nature, a vision of that quality of humanity which life in society tends to distort. In so far as they do suggest this, they are indeed humanist, and general and even universal in their scope.

This impression has been enforced by another feature which might be called self-effacement. There are many seventeenth century works in which the author delights to appear, to give his views, even about his characters. In the works we have here studied (and this is a feature often called classical) the author is concerned to keep out of his picture, to give it validity by omitting all mention of an individual point of view. When Pascal wrote his famous note 'le moi est haïssable' he meant something on these lines: that self-display should be curbed, in letters as in life. One gathers from other notes that these things were discussed in the salons and that expertise was frowned upon. Types such as Alceste, or the Arrias of La Bruyère, who preferred to hold forth rather than to listen, were clearly an object of raillery. The ideal was 'les gens universels', who did not disturb or monopolise conversation.

One has only to think of the lack of interest in historical change, the absence of any idea of relativity, notions already discussed, to see that this self-effacement was working in the same direction, and that taken together these two tendencies might well give readers the idea that the aim of 'classical' works was a didactic presentation of general and universal features. If for example the sentiments of a tragic character were not peculiar to any distinct period of history and were not (at least in expression) any revelation of the author's own view, then such drama would (if it survived) appear to be more abstract and generalised than was ever intended. This has in fact led to strange misunderstandings. Writers have been taken to intend portrayal of the general truth about human nature, when as a matter of fact there is no proof that they intended this, and some probability that they did not. Even Mr. Peyre assumes something of this kind:

Corneille et Racine recherchaient chez Rodrigue ou chez Roxane le fond éternel qui les rapprochait des Français de Louis XIV et des hommes et des femmes de tous les temps et de tous les pays.[2]

The truth may be that it never occurred to such writers to do anything else than to suggest certain human features. The question cannot be answered until we have dealt with a prior question, which is that of literary creation itself. What process goes on when any work of art is made? Does it consist in translating on to paper the intentions of the creator, his ideas? Or is it the clothing of a vision that comes to the artist as something the reverse of abstract, something personal and particular? If the latter is the case, then the generality of French classical work may be a myth. 'La création est pour elle-même une

[2] H. Peyre, *Le Classicisme français*, 1942, p. 78. See also some interesting pages by H. Levin in *Contexts of Criticism*, 1957, pp. 38–54.

activité assez obscure . . . On ne sait quel décalage, dou-
loureux ou ironique, existe entre les intentions de l'auteur
et la vérité de sa création . . . à peine prennent-ils la plume
qu'une force mystérieuse dévie leur main: l'œuvre se
substitue à la sincérité . . . la *Préface de Cromwell* n'est pas
la préface de *Cromwell*.'[3] We do not know, we can only
guess, how *Polyeucte* and *Tartuffe* were written, and how
closely they correspond to the intentions of their creator.
Behind every work here analysed there is probably a
particular occasion, an actual experience. An intention to
generalise or to express truths that all would admit to be
valid, that is more doubtful. But we have emphasised the
latter at the expense of the former. We may thus have
missed the essential life that is in French classical works.
As Mr. Peyre says 'A force de voir en eux la largeur
universelle et abstraite, nous les avons dépouillés d'une
grande partie de leur vérité concrète et de leur intensité
de vie' (op. cit. p. 79). There can surely be no greater
mistake than to take for didactic what was full of life and
form. Hence the necessity for a new insistence on form, on
close study of the way a work is set out, arranged, what it
says, in what order, what it omits. It is form that makes
Tartuffe compelling to those who are not interested in
hypocrisy, *Les Provinciales* and *Les Pensées* fascinating to
those far from their doctrinal position, *Les Caractères*
exciting to read for those of us who have no hope of being
improved (in La Bruyère's sense) by their morality. If we
must find a principle behind all such writing let us take it
from Boileau's Longinus and not from his *Art Poétique*:
the finest literature he says has an effect of elevation and of
transport.

The Boileau who wrote this is not the Boileau of whom

³ Gaetan Picon, *L'Ecrivain et son Ombre*, p. 14.

the textbooks speak. It is a man who started a tempestuous career by writing violent satires, the first forms of which have been recently recovered, who spent some years translating the Greek text of Longinus, issued it, and re-issued it, alongside the *Art Poétique* with an important preface, that he twice enlarged. A man who in old age seems to have been concerned to build up his own legend of the lawgiver of Parnassus, and whom the eighteenth century increasingly treated as such. Recent work has shown this interpretation to be quite unnecessary. In his conversation and in his satires he says more pungent things than the clichés of the *Art Poétique*. There is no evidence that he considered this work his chief critical production. It was received at the time as a 'succès de salon' because of its brilliant verses. We can enjoy the verses without making them into principles of esthetics.

Boileau in fact, as recent study has progressively revealed him, is an interesting Janus-like figure. Not perhaps a great writer himself, he became an immense force in European literature, in two directions. His *Art of Poetry* supplied what a prosaic age could take of poetic precept. His *Longinus* started the long discussion of the Sublime, which through Marmontel and Burke was a formative factor in Romanticism. And his *Lutrin*, most popular of all in the eighteenth century, and perhaps his best work, spread a critical attitude to epic and a taste for ironic parody, which through Pope became a vogue of English writing.

One quality which Boileau shares with his greater literary contemporaries is that of crisp formulation of picture or idea; hence his many frequently quoted lines. After study of such works as we have been here concerned with, what remains in the mind is not their insight or morality so much as such crisp and sharp pictures, either in the form of dramatic characters—Sganarelle, Argan, Chrysale, or Mithridate, Acomat, Hippolyte, Joad—or no less sharp pictures: Pascal's man in a dungeon, or his Jesuit confident in a travesty of the faith, La Rochefoucauld's barbed vignette of Retz, Saint-Simon's Achille Harlay, and many another. Pictures of antagonisms, of heart and mind, of vice and virtue, of self-interest and altruism, of the gap between speech and thought. Pictures of distortion, in man and in society: the raging and contradictory humanity of Harpagon is as vivid in our minds as the violence and cruelty of French society in the pages of Saint-Simon.

In the light of a later esthetic, this effort to give clear expression to elusive human forces was bound to appear oratorical and artificial:

L'esprit classique ne méconnaissait pas l'existence des passions violentes et des frénésies. Mais pour les peindre il voulait les comprendre, en donner une image ordonnée et claire. Sous la confusion apparente il prétendait toujours retrouver la logique cachée. La philosophie nouvelle affirme au contraire que cette explication est une déformation, cette logique un illogisme. Le caractère essentiel de la passion est d'échapper à toute raison.[4]

Despite the authority behind this view it would seem to be more true of classical tragedy than of the prose writers considered in the course of this essay. Very little, in fact, of the French writing usually called classical has the 'usual' classical qualities. Very little of it, surely, is impersonal, clear, rational, universal, or abstract. Let us by all means keep the name classical for the remarkable group

[4] D. Mornet, op. cit. p. 99.

of artists, who, though in no way a 'school', wrote from a similar standpoint and within a specifically French and seventeenth-century framework. May we not call them classical because they showed a common power to create literature which was not limited to that framework? Their writing is classical writing at least in this, that it has kept its attraction long after the conditions of its age have disappeared.

Some sources of this abiding attraction may I think be discerned. Its insistence on form as the condition of literary expression. Its discovery of the complexity within behaviour, and of the forces hostile to reason, both within and beyond human control. Its awareness of the difference between idea and act, appearance and reality, thought and action. And finally its refusal to be dogmatic or didactic, seen in its preference for pictures, cases, fictions, over arguments and admonitions. But this is to say no more than that it is truly literature, that is the work of artists rather than theorists.

Thus understood, French classical literature is a body of writing which includes more than those who agree with Boileau. The letters of Mme de Sévigné and the pictures of Retz and Saint-Simon belong to it no less than the vignettes of La Bruyère and the epigrams of La Rochefoucauld. But it does not include all, or even most, of the writing that pleased the age. It excludes the work of a practising craftsman of the theatre such as Rotrou, of so successful a novelist as Mlle de Scudéry. Personally I would find the word 'classical' difficult to use about writing so gifted as that of Fénelon. All these seem to us now, after the lapse of time, to have been without the creative and plastic power that makes literature endure.

For us it is not a question of explaining, or of fixing

categories and including the right people, so much as of understanding and enjoying powerful writing. There has perhaps been too much 'explaining' on the part of university teachers, particularly in this field. The so-called classical Age of French literature is not clear, not easy to account for, not what generations of schoolchildren have been told that it is. It is rather the very sophisticated product of 'une époque dont toute l'étrangeté, l'extrême originalité nous échappent, tant nous sommes apprivoisés dès l'enfance avec son langage et son ordonnance imposante.'[5]

On any final judgement of this literature one feels that its self-imposed limitations were a part of its strength. They enabled writers to express what otherwise has never been expressed, to convey insights which later techniques of writing could not portray. Only in the seventeenth century perhaps was it possible to convey some sense of a new world of science alongside the medieval inheritance which was able to see men and their motives in an eternal setting. We may still find, beneath the ornament and the artificial language, discoveries, and insights which only a powerful imagination could reveal. French prisoners in Silesia during the last war, lacking study materials, turned back to their classics, asking themselves what it was in *Phèdre* that seemed to them at once so beautiful and so permanent. They decided that the poet had used an old legend to express something about human choices and human limits, that he had told an old tale as a means of penetrating into mysteries. They found in the play an expression of 'le désespoir de la connaissance', a suggestion of inscrutable elements in the human make-up which, when thus objectified in a mythical figure, did not

[5] P. Valéry, *Voltaire*, 1944, p. 6.

depress, but tended to clarify and to cleanse one's view of the hidden things of human nature: 'A proprement parler la tragédie de Racine est une descente de chacun dans sa ville intérieure, une exploration des déserts et des carrefours, une battue de monstres.'[6]

[6] A. Hoog, *Littérature en Silésie*, 1950. p. 55.

INDEX

(Initials not given for well-known writers)